PUT UP & SHUT UP!

The 90's so far in cartoons with text by Hubie Bauch

LITTLE, BROWN AND COMPANY (CANADA) LIMITED

Boston • New York • Toronto • London

Copyright © 1994 by Terry Mosher and Hubert Bauch

First published by Robert Davies Publishing
This edition published in 1998 by Little, Brown and Company (Canada) Limited.

Aislin (a.k.a. Terry Mosher) lives in downtown Montreal, working as a political cartoonist for *The Gazette*. He is the father of two daughters: Aislinn and Jessica.

Hubert Bauch (a.k.a. Hubie) lives in downtown Montreal, working as a political writer for *The Gazette*. He is the father of two daughters: Dominique and Jessica.

Put Up & Shut Up! is Aislin's 25th book, Bauch's first.

Cover design and photo illustration by Mary Hughson/Editorial meeting photograph by Tedd Church

OTHER BOOKS BY AISLIN:

Aislin—100 Caricatures (1971)
Hockey Night in Moscow (1972, with Jack Ludwig)
Aislin—150 Caricatures (1973)
The Great Hockey Thaw (1974, with Jack Ludwig)
'Ello Morgentaler? Aislin—150 Caricatures (1975)
O.K. Everybody Take a Valium! Aislin—150 Caricatures (1977)
L'Humour d'Aislin (1977)
The Retarded Giant (1977, with Bill Mann)
The Hecklers: A History of Canadian Political Cartooning (1979, with Peter Desbarats)
The Year the Expos Almost Won the Pennant (1979, with Brodie Snyder)
Did the Earth Move? Aislin—180 Caricatures (1980)
The Year the Expos Finally Won Something (1981, with Brodie Snyder)
The First Great Canadian Sports Trivia Quiz Book (1981, with Brodie Snyder)

Stretchmarks (1982)
The Anglo Guide to Survival in Quebec (1983, with various Montreal writers)
Tootle: A Children's Story (1984, with Johan Sarrazin)
Where's the Trough? (1985)
Oh, Canadians! Hysterically Historical Rhymes (1986, with Gordon Snell)
Old Whores (1987)
What's the Big Deal? Questions and Answers on Free Trade (1988, with Rick Salutin)
The Lawn Jockey (1989)
Parcel of Rogues (1990, with Maude Barlow)
Barbed Lyres, Canadian Venomous Verse (1990, with various Canadian poets)
Drawing Bones—15 Years of Cartooning Brian Mulroney (1991)
One Oar in the Water: The Nasty 90's Continued in Cartoons (1997)

Canadian Cataloguing in Publication Data
Aislin
Put up & shut up: the 90's so far in cartoons

ISBN 0-316-03871-7

1. Canada—Politics and government—1993— -Caricatures and cartoons.*
2. Canada—Politics and government—1984—1993— - Caricatures and cartoons.*
3. Quebec (Province)—Politics and government—1985— -Caricatures and cartoons.*
4. Canadian wit and humor, Pictorial. I. Bauch, Hubie 1946—   . II. Title: Put up and shut up: the 90's so far in cartoons.

NC1449.A37A4 1997a   971.064'7'0207   C97-932462-9

Printed and bound in Canada

Little, Brown and Company (Canada) Limited
148 Yorkville Avenue, Toronto, ON, Canada M5R 1C2   10 9 8 7 6 5 4 3 2 1

CONTENTS

Cartoonist's Intro...

"In politics, they play a lot more dirty than hockey."
—Guy Lafleur
(after a brief stint campaigning for the YES side during the recent Canadian constitutional referendum).

Politics have replaced hockey as Canada's national game—perhaps our only indigenous activity that hasn't been a victim of an attempted foreign takeover. But then, outsiders don't understand our politics, never mind care. And there's no potential profit in it.

What a delight being a spectator (provided with a free pass and allowed to razz all sides) to Canbec's endless, rhetorical game, and being well paid for it to boot. Nevertheless, amongst my confreres up in the gondola press box, there do seem to be fewer fellow gadflys these days.

Approaching the mid-point of the decade, I thought to produce the first of three collections of cartoons on the subject of the (so far) grunge 1990s; and that these books should have a running commentary, written by someone sharing my raffish point of view. This narrowed the field considerably in these earnest, politically corrected times, so I sought out an old pal, Hubie Bauch, hiding back there in the Laissez-les-bons-temps-rouler Lounge.

When I first met Hubie, in the early '70s, we were often picked the least likely to succeed by fellow journalists (many of whom have moved on to careers in PR, political flackery, nurturing or—worst of all—television). Surprising even ourselves, we've proved survivors.

For example, during last year's federal elec-

Brian Mulroney, Aislin et Hubie Bauch in a rare appearance at The Montreal Gazette's *editorial board meeting*

tion campaign, Bauch was escorted off Kim Campbell's plane as their dogs had sniffed out some untoward substance in Hubie's Mexican *serape* luggage. While filling out his report, the arresting officer asked Bauch the correct spelling of marijuana (CP missed a classic headline on this one: DOGS CAN SMELL, BUT MOUNTIES CAN'T SPELL).

Bauch was given an obligatory slap-on-the-wrist two-week suspension by the powers that be at our newspaper,

Unpublished

and then put back to work. He is, after all, the best political writer *The Gazette* has at present.

And, Hubie survived—Kim didn't.

Most of the cartoons in this book appeared in the *Montreal Gazette*, with many others drawn for the *Toronto Star* during an experimental two-year period when I split my time between both cities, vainly trying to serve two masters in two markets.

However, my wife Carol is from Quebec City and has never been much enamoured with *les Torontois* and—when push came to shove—I returned to Montreal for good, where *The Gazette* continues to put up with my smoking (in cartoons and otherwise).

I'd like to see more editorial cartoons in colour, and have done just that with many of my favourites in this book, hoping my editors will take note.

Lastly, people always ask me: Do your cartoons ever get killed?

Indeed they do, and the reader will find several that were scattered throughout the book, identified as being *Unpublished* (as with the one above, drawn during Hubie Bauch's ignoble suspension).

So, happy hunting until our second volume on the 1990s appears in 1997, if we survive that long...

Terry Mosher (Aislin)
Montreal, July 1994

Extract from nuisance weed might kill alcohol craving: study

ASSOCIATED PRESS

WASHINGTON – Kudzu, an imported nuisance weed that often chokes trees in southern U.S. forests, might contain extracts that conquer the craving for alcohol, a study shows.

Researchers at Harvard Medical School, intrigued by the ancient Chinese use of the kudzu roots to treat alcoholism, tested compounds from the plant on a group of hard-drinking hamsters and found that the rodents went on the wagon.

Dr. Bert Vallee of the Harvard Medical School said the kudzu extract "has been used widely in Chi...

...ster. Vallee said this animal has the unique characteristic of having a huge appetite for alcohol.

The study is to be published today in the Proceedings of the National Academy of Sciences.

MORE KUDZU WEED FOR HUBIE, OUR DESIGNATED DRIVER!

Maybe if I smoked it...

It's the world's gone crazy, Cotillion
Ladies are dancing alone
The side men all want to be front men
And the front men all want to go home

The Johnny-come-latelies are coming in early
The early birds showing up late
The straight men all want to be funny
And the funny ones want to get straight

Villains are turned into heroes
Heroes are turned into heels
The dealers all want to be lovers
And the lovers all want to make deals

The meek, they inherited nothing
Leaders are gone in the night
So I'm singing my song to the deaf men
And doing my dance for the blind*

* (Shel Silverstein & Waylon Jennings; BMI)

It's unlikely that any of the boys in the Sûreté du Québec riot squad were familiar with that little ditty by Shel Silverstein, though it would have made as good a marching song for them as any that fateful morning in July, 1990 when they donned their kevlar underwear in their grim downtown fortress on Parthenais St. and headed forth into battle, to a little town off the western tip of Montreal Island called Oka. If not a marching song, then a cautionary tale, for their world was about to be turned upside down.

There was a rash of gin-fed salon talk at the tail end of the '80s about the end of history. Now that the collapse of the evil commie empire had cleared the way for the worldwide triumph of liberal democracy, there wouldn't be any need for new wars as the planet inexorably settled into a new millennium of moo-cow *gemütlichkeit*, in which everyone would, in due time, gain access to one-stop shopping, fast food and automated banking. Forty years' worth of stockpiled ICBMs with nuclear warheads had suddenly become as useful to the pursuit of geo-politics—for all but outlaw biker countries like North Korea and Iraq—as a warehouse packed to the rafters with spare parts for Studebaker sedans.

Alas, the human species hadn't yet evolved to the point where boys of all ages no longer require an application for their aggressive genes. So come the '90s we had to make do with new takes on old wars: religious wars, tribal wars, civil wars and desert wars in backwater locales like Somalia, Yugoslavia, Rwanda and Kuwait, places where major arms manufacturers and members of the Trilateral Commission don't have vacation homes. Here in Canada, in keeping with the spirit of the times, we turned back the clock and had us an Indian war. Granted, it was unlike any Indian war we've seen or heard about, in the movies or the history books.

Generations of grade-school Canadians' minds

had been conditioned to believe that Samuel de Champlain did the right and good thing in his first encounter with representatives of the Iroquois confederacy when he reputedly scattered one of their war parties with a single volley from his trusty blunderbuss; any ambiguity on that score would have elicited a failing grade on the final exam. This time, both sides got equal time to hold up their side on prime time TV as the story was unfolding, so public opinion was challenged by starkly contrasting versions of the tale from the outset.

For many, the Mohawk warriors who threw up the barricades across the road at Oka and the Mercier Bridge—one of the major spans linking Montreal with the mainland—were noble defenders of an oppressed indigenous people, their backs pushed to the wall by the affronts of a racist white society. For just as many others, they were nothing more than trigger-happy gunsels for the Mohawk mafia, whose main concern was protecting the illicit cigarette traffic and outlaw gambling operations on their reserves. Anyone groping for middle ground was ruthlessly slagged

SOME WARRIOR...

MAFIA APPROVED

AISLIN 90
MONTREAL
THE GAZETTE

by the true believers on both sides.

There wasn't that much more in the way of actual gunplay this time either, considering that during the interval both sides had achieved rough parity in firestick technology. (The actual shooting was over in minutes, but there was enough to cost QPF Cpl. Marcel Lemay his life. As the standoff settled into a war of nerves and public-relations strategies—in which it got ever more difficult to tell the heroes from the villains—he became the forgotten man of the episode. An inquest into his death was launched much later, and at this writing has been going on for close to twice as long as the Oka crisis itself. Judging from the testimony rendered so far, they seem no more likely to come up with with Cpl. Lemay's killer than with Jimmy Hoffa's corpse or the trick to getting the filling into Caramilk bars.)

There may have been nothing funny about Cpl. Lemay's death, and a lot of people still fail to see any humour in the Oka Crisis at all, starting with those who lived within the battle lines and had their homes ransacked and vandalized, and then got jerked around by the

The Mayor of Oka

The absent Cabinet Ministers

government over promised compensation. But in just about every other way it was a surrealist's picnic, not to mention a cartoonist's field day.

If it wasn't like anything in the conventional history texts, neither was it *Dances With Wolves*. An Indian war for the '90s, if Oka is anything to go by, lends itself more readily to theatre of the absurd than epic cinema.

It would have to be about something weirdly ridiculous like, say . . . a golf course. Yeah, that's it . . . a scruffy nine-holer in a little bedroom town in Quebec, whose previous claim to renown had been its Trappist monastery, where the monks had concocted a brand of cheese renowned for its rich nose of toejam and pronounced aftertaste of old socks. The call to arms would be sounded in a flash of megalomania by the local mayor, while the minister supposedly in charge of the provincial police force is off working on a tan. The federal minister in charge of native affairs would be the reigning cabinet klutz, whose idea of The Great Spirit is Seagram's Crown Royal.

In this movie, the forces of law and order would proceed to make Frank Drebin and his *Naked Gun* cohorts look like Elliott Ness and the Untouchables. Having gone to the barricades to thwart the expansion of the golf course on what they claimed as their sacred ground, triumphant Mohawk warriors—decked out in combat fatigues, with kerchief masks tied across their noses and loaded guns slung over their shoulders—would hit the links themselves the next day to cavort for the network cameras, flailing about with drivers on the tees and running golf-cart races down the fairways and over the greens. The Indians would have evocative names, redolent of their noble tradition—like Lasagna, Noriega and Mad Jap.

If it hadn't actually happened that way, even the most venturesome producer would have rejected this script as just too sideways for popular consumption, even by people who claim to understand what *The Piano* was all about, or find redeeming virtues in the Jerry Lewis œuvre.

There were people on both sides of the barricades that strange summer who thought at times that the world had gone crazy, and none more so than the members of Quebec's provincial police force, whose major function, under normal circumstances, is to bust excessively flagrant speeders on intercity autoroutes and break up barfights in jerkwater towns that can't afford their own constabulary. In the world that the QPF troopers knew up to then, it had rarely taken more than a show of numbers and a whiff of tear gas to clear a native barricade.

Not only did they get shot at this time, but they took a casualty, and several of their cars got trashed in the bargain; to rub it in, the Mohawks used the cop car wrecks to shore up their barricade. Their political masters, paralyzed by the thought of a bloodbath that would smear Canada's schoolboy image abroad, ordered the police into a holding pattern. They had to stand by and watch as learned judges, front-bench cabinet ministers and the prime minister's personal representative sat down to

negotiate respectfully with these masked Rambo-wannabe punks, as though they were diplomatic emissaries from a major trading partner. To them it was like an FBI delegation doing lunch in Little Italy with John Gotti.

Though standard procedure calls on them to deal ungently with armed punks blocking traffic on major arteries, they actually wound up protecting the Mohawk barricades from mobs of outraged citizens spoiling to take the law into their own hands. All summer long they were taunted by a capsule summary of their bungled attack, writ large in Day-Glo orange spray paint on a cement block at the base of the Oka barricade: "They came, they saw, they ran." The only outlet they could find for their mounting frustration was to club sideline protesters, intimidate journalists and harrass non-combatant natives trying to go about their daily business. Both the pro- and anti-native elements in the peanut gallery agreed on one thing: the cops were blowing it badly.

News Item: Chateauguay's White Warriors have some difficulty setting Indian effigy on fire

...OR YOU COULD RUB TWO STICKS TOGETHER ...AND PRAY.

Their injured pride was ground in salt by the media coverage of the crisis, in which the cops came off as either clueless fumblers or ham-fisted provocateurs. Columnists made cruel references to the storied cop fondness for doughnuts, and lead editorials loftily demanded they be yanked off the case. A video by a popular comedy troupe, in heavy rotation on the local pop music channel that summer, lampooned the QPF as a bunch of lardassed cryptonazis, and a leading hotline host dubbed them The Little Pinochets.

What finally made them snap was an Aislin cartoon of a big hairy-faced mutt wearing shades and a police hat with a doughnut insignia on the badge, bearing the motto: "Chien Chaud." It provoked a bizarre communiqué, faxed out of QPF headquarters in the dead of night, accusing the English media, and _The Gazette_ in particular, of disseminating raw Mohawk propaganda, and of harbouring an anti-police bias because the Meech Lake constitutional deal fell through.

16

It was the PR equivalent of tossing tear gas cannisters upwind, which is what the riot squad apparently did that disastsrous first morning at Oka, according to the scuttlebutt on the cop grapevine. All it did was draw wider attention to the offending caricature, and provide the offending cartoonist with more ammunition, not to mention a chance to cavort shamelessly in his sudden notoriety. Though no one could quite figure out what Meech Lake had to do with any of this, the police force was righteously flayed in both the French and English papers for presuming to level political charges against a pillar of the free press. No matter which way they turned, the shit-fan blew in their faces.

doned the barricades, but it appeared to be mostly for form, and less violent than an average period of NHL hockey.

The fallout from that Oka summer is still coming down in the courts and by way of sporadic low-level skirmishing between the cops and the Indians on the fringes of the local reserves. Some leaders from then have disappeared into the night, and some who were sidemen now hold centre stage. The optimists said the good thing about the Oka fiasco was that it would focus attention on native issues, and lead to greater understanding and the redressment of longstanding grievances, as though this surreal episode could settle into a remake of Pollyanna. But like the rest of humanity, neither side in this lingering standoff seems to have greatly changed its nature.

News items: Government lowers taxes on cigarettes to put an end to smuggling...

After all else had failed, the authorities resorted to convention: they called in the cavalry. The standoff finally ended after several weeks of both sides rattling weaponry at each other and trying to frighten the enemy with withering grimaces. There was some pushing and shoving when the last holdouts aban-

As such, the sequel to the Oka drama could break out at any time. If it does, the only certainty is that it'll be even more absurd.

Please help the police track down this heinous **CARTOONIST ON THE LAM!**

J'AI TROUVÉ LE CARICATURISTE!

No stranger to the police, *Monsieur Toon* has been seen at 5 a.m. in Dunkin Donut planning new & devious cartoons!

This cartoonist, one of the 10 most wanted, lurks in front of Cantor's reading *The Sunday New York Times!*

Road blocks won't stop this desparado!

YOU'RE GOING 18 kph... AND THIS ISN'T TORONTO!

OKAY. SHOULD I SLOW DOWN?

Desparate, he will kidnap his own cats and *Moll*, holing up in his lower Westmount cottage!

HEY, WE'LL PHONE OUT FOR ALL OUR FOOD...AND THEN HAVE 10 or 15 VIDEOS SENT OVER...

With no air conditioning?

NO PROBLEM! THEY DELIVER, DON'T THEY?

AISLIN '91 MONTREAL THE GAZETTE

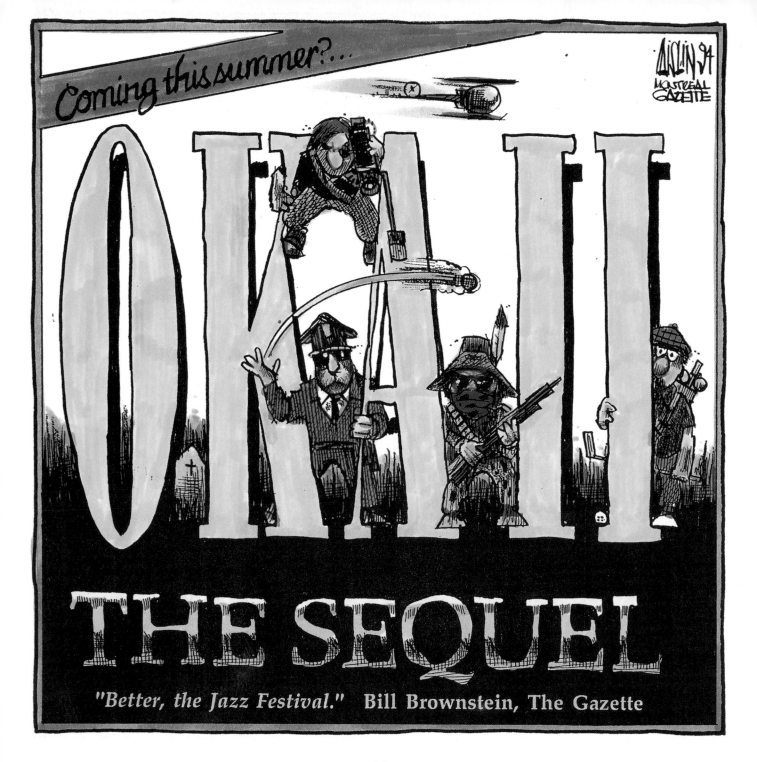

22

Chapter 2: Québec after Bourassa?

A lot of people who thought they knew Robert Bourassa well were convinced that he'd never leave the Quebec premier's office under his own steam; that he'd either have to be carried out by six in a pine box, or be given the heave by six million in a provincial election, in which case it would be only a matter of time before he'd be back. It was said of Bourassa that there were only two things in life that held any compelling interest for him: being premier of Quebec and, failing that, scheming to become premier of Quebec. It was widely held that Sheila Copps would join an order of cloistered nuns and take a vow of silence, or that Jean Chrétien would take up playing Shakespeare on the main stage at Stratford, before Robert Bourassa would walk away from politics.

When the '90s began, he was heading into the second term of his second coming, and had his brush with cancer not rearranged his world view, he'd surely have completed it and contested the next election. At the time of his departure in September of 1993, the polls suggested that the voters had once again tired of his face, and wanted a change so desperately they were prepared to put up with Jacques Parizeau as premier. But who was to say he wouldn't try again after that? And, who knows, maybe even win again. Those who knew him best always said that as long as he could walk, he'd be running for premier. And for all his alleged other faults, it's been something at which he was better than anyone in Quebec since Maurice Duplessis owned the franchise. The record will forever show that the greatly maligned "Bou-Bou" won twice as many elections as the sainted René Lévesque, and that he beat Lévesque's party four times while they locked in on his number just once.

His first comeback was sufficiently improbable to make anything seem possible. Remember, here was a guy who'd been described by one of his own caucus members as the most hated man in the province without eliciting much in the way of a rebuke from anyone, not even the boss himself, who'd probably heard it often enough already from his pollster. After his government got blown away by the PQ in the 1976 Quebec election shocker, the prospect of a Robert Bourassa revival was generally regarded as somewhat less likely than a papal wedding, a Pat Paulsen presidency or little green men landing on the corner of Peel and St. Catherine in a spaceship piloted by Amelia Earhart. By getting himself elected premier again nine years later, he pulled off one of the most spectacular comebacks in Canadian politics since Confederation. To top it, the Tories would have to storm back to power with a crushing majority two federal elections hence—with Brian Mulroney as their leader.

What was long the most famous line about Robert Bourassa, was written early in his career by that most sublimely literate of Quebec journalists, Jean-V. Dufresne, who compared him to an underfed credit union accountant. (Contrary to prevailing myth, Pierre Trudeau never actually called him a hot-dog eater in so many words, but it remains a strong runner-up in public perception.) Twenty years later, after Bourassa had proven himself one of the great political survivors in Quebec history, Dufresne summed him up as the classic case of a walking ambiguity. "Where Trudeau was all plane geometry, the pure esthetic of the straight line, Bourassa is the luxuriant arabesque of the pretzel. It leads nowhere and everywhere at the same time." (In keeping with the pastry analogy, could it be said that Jacques Parizeau is the puffy circumference defining the hollow core of a doughnut?) Where Trudeau would sting like a bee, Bourassa would float like a butterfly. If Trudeau was a falcon, as one biographer cast him, striking fear in his prey with talons of steel, then Bourassa was a cuckoo, sowing confusion in the federal flock as he flitted from one nest to another. Aislin got about as close to capturing the essential Robert Bourassa as ever, in 20 years of trying, with a cartoon that had him chiding the pundits for calling him a fence hugger. "I never stand on the fence," Aislin's Bourassa declares. "I am the fence."

And what a crooked fence he was, zigging this way and that, like a constituency line after several generations of artful gerrymandering. Until very late in his career—some would say

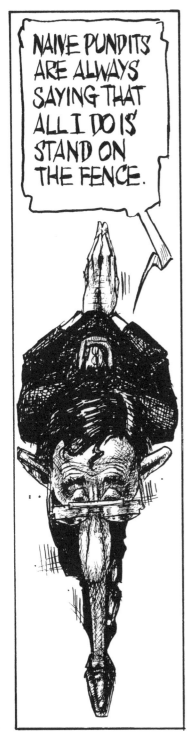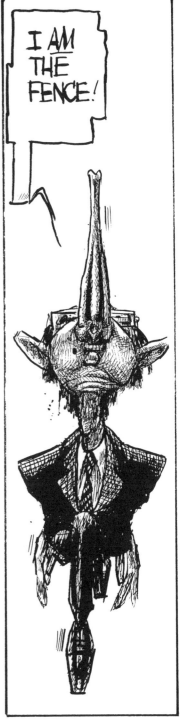

too late—no one could quite figure out if he was a committed federalist or a closet separatist. Or if he was a genius or a fool; a master strategist worthy of Machiavelli, or a misguided sorcerer's apprentice befitting Mickey Mouse. When he put his mind to it, he could shred the separatist argument as effectively as anyone, yet he seemed to find it painfully difficult to declare himself a heartfelt federalist. It was as though the unqualified, un-appended term would stick in his throat like a chicken bone when he tried to speak its name, sort of like Don Cherry trying to say something positive about a Swede who just scored a hat trick in a playoff game against the Bruins.

When pressed about his constitutional preference, he'd grope for misty euphemisms and weasel metaphors, like a high church pre-late trying to describe a particularly kinky sexual practice. He was far more comfortable with swivelhipped catchphrases, like profitable federalism, cultural sovereignty, the Canadian common market and the distinct society, to describe his vision of Quebec's place in Canada. When it came to constitutional affairs, he seemed to regard Confederation as a cruising bar in which he could swing both ways. It was as though he built his career on standup comic Yvon Deschamps's line that what the Québécois have really wanted all along is an independent Quebec in a united Canada.

Well into the '90s he mused openly about some kind of federal superstructure arrangement modelled after the European Union, and he encouraged his party to endorse the quasi-separatist

Mordecai Richler's Quebec piece appears in the New Yorker

Allaire Report, under which the federal government would be largely reduced to running the post office, printing money and handing out equalization payments. At times he caved in to the nationalists, as when he reneged on the Victoria Charter in 1971, which could have spared us all a lot of constitutional expense and ennui. And at times he led them down the garden path, as he did after the Meech Lake accord fell through 20 years later, when he had some of them convinced that he was about to hijack the sovereignty bus and drive it all the way to independence. Instead, he got bogged down in Charlottetown, where all this constitutional nonsense started in the first place; talk about working yourself into a pretzel.

Bourassa announces his retirement

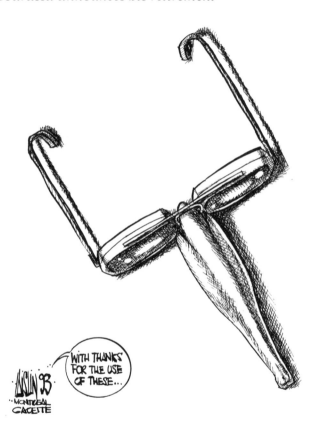

WITH THANKS FOR THE USE OF THESE...

Much the same jellyfish ambiguity, and sheer head-banging frustration, coloured Bourassa's roller-coaster relationship with Quebec's English community, which, during the span of his years in politics, has gone from master race to endangered species. Though French has never been more widely spoken in Quebec, and most English Quebecers are now functionally bilingual, the nationalists are dead reluctant to let the old squarehead bogey limp off to the boneyard where it belongs. They've found that nothing gooses the PQ's polling numbers like a good wave of linguistic paranoia, provoked by some pinhead sociology professor doing a little sleight-of-hand with the census numbers, or some backwater town council in deepest Ontario passing an English-only bylaw. In the Quebec of the 1990s, unilingual francophones earn more than bilingual anglophones, yet in popular Québécois myth, the average anglo remains a composite of Colonel Blimp and Simon Legree, who lives in a palatial Westmount mansion bought with the sweat of his Québécois wage slaves.

English Quebecers looked to Bourassa as their saviour from the separatist menace when

he first became premier, not long after the first outbreaks of language turmoil in the late '60s. Yet he betrayed them not once but twice. The first time was when he brought in Bill 22, the first language legislation giving English official secondary status in Quebec, then again when he made his comeback in the mid-'80s, by promising to rescind the PQ law banning English from shop signs. When the time came for him to deliver, the nationalist backlash approached thermonuclear proportions, replete with apocalyptic prophesies that with such en-

couragement, the Anglo-Saxon hordes wouldn't rest until the last mom and pop steamie joint in Pointe-aux-Trembles is crowned with golden arches. Badly rattled, Bourassa tried to make everybody happy with his patented recipe for half-baked fudge: he allowed some English on store signs, but only indoors—as though English is some kind of virulent bacterial strain activated by exposure to daylight.

This time, it was the anglos who went ballistic. The agitated rattling of teacups rolled like thunder down the western slope of Mount Royal; little old ladies traded in their tennis shoes for hobnailed boots, and Holt Renfrew's stocked designer combat fatigues. At the Westmount Library, there was a run on Henry David Thoreau by people who normally regard John Stuart Mill as subversive, and in the 1989 provincial election, they voted heavily for a raggedy-ass anglo rights group called the Equality Party, which won four National Assembly seats in Montreal's predominantly English west end.

Since then, the greatest service the Equality Party has rendered to the body politic in Quebec has been to demonstrate conclusively to francophones that the blokes are really no longer a threat to anyone but themselves. By the time the next election loomed, three of its four Assembly members, including founding leader Robert Libman, had either pulled out of the party or been purged. After four years of fratricidal bloodletting that made the Borgias look like the Brady Bunch, the party had alienated all but its bedrock element of obses-

EQUALITY PARTY ELECTS 4...

Merde...

A SURVIVOR

1960s...

1970s...

1980s...

1990s...

Equality Party leader Robert Libman

Quebec law eases restrictions on English usage slightly

sive anglo rights cranks, who tend to be about as reasonable and endearing as the franco language hysterics. (The Eeks, as they became known in the local argot, turned out to be a classic example of the political rule of thumb which holds that the more insignificant a party's chances of taking power, the more vicious the infighting within its ranks.) As one local wag noted, if the doomsayers on both sides of the language divide are right, there won't be any anglos left in Quebec 10 years from now, but everyone in the province will speak nothing but English.

Equality caucus renegade Richard Holden administered the ultimate insult to the anglo community's battered dignity when he crossed the floor of the National Assembly to sit with the PQ as the separatist member for Westmount, though up to then he had little more in common with Jacques Parizeau than Jackie Gleason's belt size, Teddy Kennedy's libido, and a bosom friendship with Johnny Walker. On the Canadian scale of treachery, it was akin to Stompin' Tom Connors moving to Las Vegas to front a Kenny Rogers cover band, or Maude Barlow running off to Cleveland with the chairman of the Amex Bank.

Things polarized quickly in Quebec in the wake of Robert Bourassa's departure. Under his successor, Daniel Johnson, the Liberals struck a more resolutely federalist pose than at any time during the past three decades. After shunning the term like a case of the crabs for the longest time, Jacques Parizeau frankly admitted that he's a separatist. It cleared the way for what looms as the decisive clash between federalist and separatist forces in Quebec, with all its poten-

Maverick EP member Richard Holden switches to the PQ

NEWS ITEM: JACQUES PARIZEAU WAS SEEN WALKING HIS DOG IN WESTMOUNT...

NON, NON, RICHARD! I SAID, "SIT!"

Starting Today!

Laurel & Hardy in
The Battle for Québec

A NUMBER OF FAITHFUL READERS HAVE EXPRESSED SOME CONCERN OVER WHAT THIS SPACE WILL EVER DO WITHOUT ROBERT BOURASSA, AFTER HE RETIRES...

DON'T WORRY ...BE HAPPY

Daniel Johnson

tially ruinous consequences. The day may yet come when both sides in the current debate will wish the fence was still in place.

NEWS ITEM: BOUCHARD REMAINS TWICE AS POPULAR AS PARIZEAU IN QUEBEC POLLS…

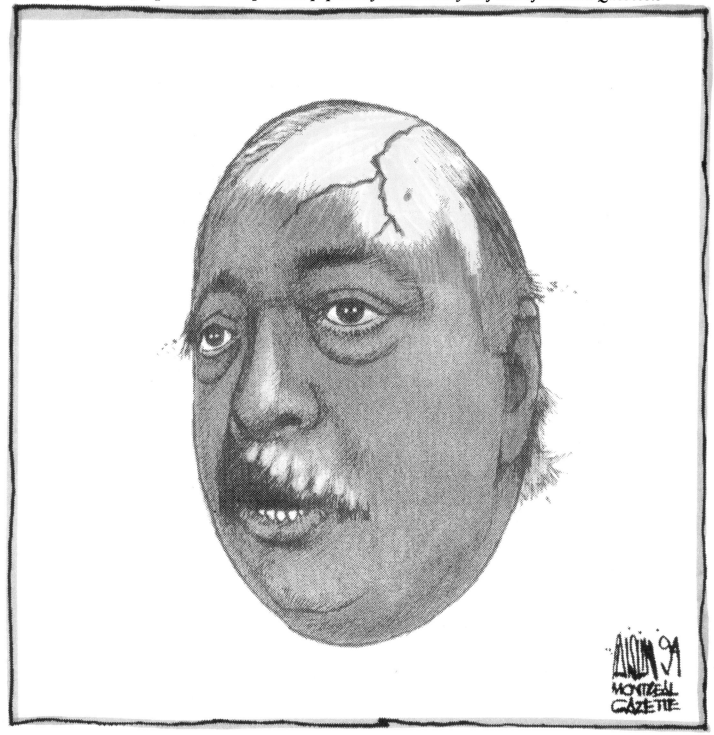

41

Chapter 3: Montreal vs. Toronto

The constant wonder of Montreal isn't that it works as well as it does, but that it works at all. Listening to some of the blowtorch rhetoric from the fanatics on both sides of the imaginary fence between the alleged two solitudes, you'd think people would be clawing each other's eyes out on streetcorners and hurling rocks from opposite sidewalks on St. Lawrence Boulevard, the mythical dividing line between the franco East End and the anglo West Island. Yet there's nothing unduly hostile or dangerous about the streets of Montreal, except for the uninitiated who innocently venture out on them at the wheel of a car. The only riots worthy of the name during the past 20 years have been hockey related, and St. Laurent is the funkiest good-time strip in town. It's true that hard objects get thrown in anger there sometimes, but only when the cops feel the need to move in on some particularly happening party scene. If you could turn down the sound and dissolve the backdrop, and just watch people going about their daily rounds, you couldn't tell Montreal from any other big town in the country, though after a while you'd notice that these people devote an indecent amount of time and effort to the sole purpose of having fun, and you'd know for sure at least that you're not in Toronto.

Oh lord, into the cheap shots already. But what else can you expect from unreconstructable Montrealers? (Best to admit right up front that's what we are, both me and the cartoonist; we've been here so long now that you can't take us anywhere without asking for trouble, least of all down the 401.)

For hardcore Montrealers, taking the mickey out of Toronto is a cultural reflex, like ordering doubles at a quarter to three, crossing on the red and playing kissy-face in public with near strangers. It may be true that the last thing Torontonians need to hear are more smartass cracks about the Protestant work ethic—or gratuitous sneering at the Hogtown dweebs for thanking god it's Monday—from one more cirrhotic Montreal bistro layabout who doesn't know when to go home at night. But Montrealers figure it's something Toronto owes them for having it all, or being allowed to pretend it does; think of it as equalization payments of the soul.

You also have to understand that the '90s haven't been kind to Montreal so far. It may still be the city that never sleeps, but lately it's been spending a lot of nights lying awake and staring at the ceiling, wondering how much worse it has to get before it gets better. Instead of drinking to be merry, it's been drinking to forget. As the recession deepened, parts of Montreal began to take on a distinct third-world cast. Encroaching seediness started over-

bombing run. In the rutted streets, monster potholes swallowed up unwary compact vehicles. The most common advertisements in storefront windows were "Closed" and "For Sale." Designer boutiques gave way to dollar stores, and soup kitchens drew a steadier clientele than the three-star restaurants. Amid this mounting adversity, slagging Toronto was one of the things Montrealers could still cling to for a little ego lift, like threadbare old-country aristocrats sneering at the moneyed bourgeoisie whose vulgar fortunes were made in drygoods. The sidewalks in Toronto may be paved with gold, they sniff, but a damn lot of good it does if you roll them up at sundown.

Typical of the attitude is that a while back, when the Expos were being ballyhooed as the Team of the '80s, Montreal ball fans were un-

taking its fabled downtown chic at an alarming rate. Montreal may still have had its moments in the National Hockey League, but this decade it's been number one most often in the national poverty rankings and the bankruptcy statistics for major cities in the country; at times the unemployment rate in Montreal outstripped the Newfoundland percentage, seasonally adjusted or otherwise.

The downtown landscape became increasingly disfigured by the boarded-up husks of burned-out buildings left to linger in crumbling disrepeair; for a while it seemed like the only guy in town with ironclad job security was Marvin the Torch. Abandoned midtown construction projects left great gaping holes in the ground, making it look as though the city core had been the target of a misdirected NORAD

Councillor sues ex-employer for bar and food expenses

MICHELLE LALONDE
THE GAZETTE

City Councillor Nick Auf der Maur was in Quebec Court yesterday demanding that Quebecor Inc. pay $6,666 in bar and restaurant bills that he ran up in 1990.

The colorful councillor for the Peter-McGill district wrote a thrice-weekly column for a Quebecor publication, the Montreal Daily News, until it folded in December 1989.

Auf der Maur signed a contract that stipulated that if the paper stopped publishing, he would continue to receive his salary for months. He contends that a $10,000 annual allowance for travel and entertainment was part of his salary, which should have continued for months after the paper folded. His claim is for two-thirds of

"A contract is a contract," Auf

becor lawyer Antoine Tremblay said in an interview package did not provide for inclusion of the expense account.

Auf der Maur, the city councillor for

SO — IF I DROP THE $6 FOR FOOD, WILL YOU SETTLE OUT OF COURT?

...ndness for doing ...d restaurants.
...olitical contacts ...stituents regularly ...Bar on Bishop St ...d to talk to the ...Maur himself
...ng as a ...when ...hired ...ry of

...ave ...ole ...ny

stories, Auf der Maur said.

45

sparing in their condescension toward Toronto and the Blue Jays, who were an expansion franchise at the time, struggling out of the American League basement while the Expos were division contenders in what we here like to call the "senior circuit." Though the Jays have since gone on to win the World Series not once but twice in this decade, they still got no respect in Montreal. Toronto's team may have developed into the Cadillac franchise of its league while the Expos deteriorated into the team from Rent-A-Wreck, but Montreal holds nothing but disdain for the Jays as a joyless agglomeration of overpaid mercenaries whose success was solely contingent on their management's obscenely fatted wallet. The '90s Montreal attitude smugly asserted that the hardscrabble Expos—albeit of dire necessity—

Torontonians face up to hard times

played far more artful and inspirational baseball, truer to the spirit of the game etc., even as they folded pitifully in every late season stretch. Toronto's unbridled enthusiasm for its championship club was frostily deplored as just one more example of its insufferable penchant for vulgar excesses of Metro boosterism. Montrealers, of course, know how to handle such things with exemplary restraint and sophistication, which they demonstrated by trashing the main downtown shopping strip the last two times the Canadiens won the Stanley Cup.

Montrealers are also inordinately proud of their splendid jazz festival each summer, during which the city swings like no other place on earth. Yet Toronto supports a far livelier jazz scene the year round, while

Montreal hosts annual International Jazz Festival

A Toronto portfolio of cartoons...

Toronto debates how to dispose of its garbage

PAUL GODFREY'S SUNshine Girl!

JOYOUS JUNE'S JUST JAKE

SUNshine BOY! Page 184. Commie Jack Layton poses for us with his environmentally correct shower head...

HUG A COP

Win Sun stuff!

SUN SWOONS OVER JUNE!

TODAY'S WEATHER Socialist rain will continue

WEEKEND WEATHER Red fronts everywhere

TODAY'S DONUT Blue Jay Berry

Help ANDY find his bird!

ALLAN FOTHERINGHAM is on holidays but will, of course, write on it anyway...

ALSON '91 TORONTO STAR

49

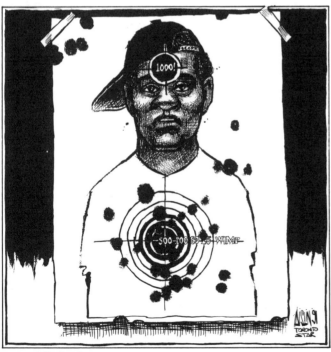

Unpublished

50

...the people in charge still seem very much the same.

Montreal jazz musicians—so trendy during those dozen party-down days each summer—live mostly in hand-to-mouth anonymity through the long winters. Montrealers like to preen about their cultural sophistication, but a recent study showed that Torontonians are, on the whole, more avid supporters of the arts. It also shattered the ultimate French-girls-are-more-fun stereotype when it noted that Toronto women tend to step out on the town more regularly than their Montreal sisters. Now if they could learn how to dress like the demoiselles on St. Denis Street … but then Montreal would have to shut up once and for all.

Bogus as it may be at times, Toronto bashing is not only a

THERE YOU GO, JOHN, PARAPHRASING VOLTAIRE AGAIN…

ROSIE DIMETRO INTERVIEWING OLERUD.

…Toronto leatherette

morale resuscitator for bruised Montreal sensibilities, but part of the social glue that holds the town together, as both English and French freely indulge with equally malicious glee. But while it remains a *divertissement* that we're not about to outgrow in the near future, the stereotypes that sustain it have been wearing increasingly thin. What the '90s have shown so far is that Montreal and Toronto are getting to have so much in common that the old rivalry is becoming downright silly.

Both have grown into sprawling metropolitan centres with much the same big city problems—and pleasures, from the high fallutin' to the downright felonious. The recession also had a brutal impact on Toronto, which felt it harder than Montreal in some ways, if only because it had more to lose and less experience at getting mugged in the corporate marketplace. The most significant development in both towns during the past quarter century has been their growing ethnic diversity. Both have been enriched by burgeoning cosmopolitanism, though at the same time it has created common problems of integration, and diluted their traditional identities. In both towns, for instance, it took the cops a while to learn that visible minorities aren't for target practice. Quebec may be a distinct society, but Montreal, even with its French fact, now has far more in common, socially and culturally, with Toronto than with Quebec City or Chicoutimi, just as any semi-hip Torontonian would surely feel far more comfortable in Montreal than in Thunder Bay or The Soo.

Most Montrealers would be affronted by the suggestion, but there are things they could learn from Toronto. Like paying closer attention to what goes on at city hall, for instance. While Toronto has gone for variety in its mayors over the years—from John Sewell on the left to June Rowlands on the right, and from tiny perfect David Crombie to perfectly bland Art Eggelton—Montrealers have had only two mayors during the past 30 years, and both have been short-legged lawyers with mustaches, whose initials are J.D. To their dismay, one turned out to be alarmingly like the other. The defining stroke of Jean Dore's administration that lodged in the minds of most Montrealers this decade is the $300,000 he spent to have an elaborate new picture window installed in his office at the height of the recession. Meanwhile, the legacy of Jean Drapeau's delusions of grandeur continues to haunt the city in the form of the Olympic Stadium—the most expensive building in the world—which has already started falling apart even though it won't be fully paid for until well into the next century. Since most of the stadium debt is being financed by cigarette taxes, anti-smoking regulations will continue to be a joke in Montreal, much like the traffic laws. Montrealers will take this as further evidence that, unlike the milkfed Toronto wussies, we really know how to live.

Still, it's becoming harder and harder for Montrealers to work up a good head of Torontophobia when there are so many good reasons to commiserate instead. Toronto's

Montréal: a city of delightful contrasts!

The PHANTOM of the OPERA

"A glorious inside peek at the self-indulgence of our mandarin class, with all its fiddling and *franchement*-ing - all the while burning our money to keep City Hall really, really warm"
Bill Marsden

Les Misér

"A compelling portrayal of the *joie de vivre* to be found in a community with the highest unemployment rate of any major North American city."
Bill Brownstein

"And, coming soon, DOGS! – featuring Gary Carter."

DID YOU KNOW THAT ONE COMPANY OFFERED THE CITY OF MONTREAL NOT ONE, BUT A PACKAGE OF *THREE*, SAFE OLYMPIC STADIUM ROOFS? AND FOR A LOT LESS THAN $47 MILLION, TOO...

Unpublished

55

stadium may have a roof that works and parts that have stayed in place so far, but we here were delighted to hear that the Skydome (or is that just plain Skydome to you, mister) has also turned out to be a sinkhole for public funds, if not quite on the Olympian scale of the "Big Owe." The low farce in high office at city hall in Montreal, where Jean Doré and his MCM administration gave serious consideration at one point to installing doggie urinals in public parks, was matched and surpassed by Bob Rae and his NDP government at Queen's Park, where the premier took time out from cooking up a new social contract for Ontario to pursue what turned out to be a mercifully aborted songwriting career, with an embarrassingly lame little ditty that nevertheless elicited a charge of plagiarism. Both Rae and Doré have served their respective communities as object lessons in the folly of letting yuppies with leftish inclinations run anything more complicated than a cheese counter.

Forget about Toronto the good and Montreal the naughty; in the '90s there are no strangers to sin. Public morality has crumbled apace in both Ontario and Quebec in this decade. Where Toronto's local pols tried to ban a pop group called the Barenaked Ladies, Montreal's tried to outlaw signs depicting barenaked ladies or parts thereof from strip club marquees. Neither bunch succeeded, just as they failed to save their respective cities from the scourge of table dancing. From there it was just a nudge down the slippery slide into the depravity of casino gambling and the sacrilege of Sunday shopping.

On the business side, both Bay St. and Quebec Inc. rang up landmark losses in the post-'80s bust, from the collapse of Lavalin to the fall of the house of Olympia and York. And while the power breakfast has supplanted the three-martini lunch in Montreal as in Toronto, it doesn't seem to have done much for the business community's performance level in either town.

Montrealers may still be a long way from embracing the Queen City cousins as kindred spirits, but it was a lot more fun kicking them when they were up, and a lot easier when their backsides didn't look so much like ours.

It should also be acknowledged that Montrealers aren't the only ones who get their existential jollies from putting the hobnails to Toronto. From Bonavista-Twillingate to Esquimault-Metchosin, one of the critical bonding agents that holds this quarrelsome country

Oh, COMMÉ ÇI, COMME ÇA...

SOLIDARITY

The only logical explanation is that after 40 years under the brogue heel of Tory dominion, Ontarians were recklessly determined to sample all the alternatives, like Weight Watchers flunkouts at a smorgasbord. It took them roughly one tenth that time to tire of the Liberals and David Peterson, the first Canadian premier to be constructed entirely by TV consultants from colour charts, fabric swatches and computerized hairstyle samples. They'd tried the Red Tie, so why not the Red Tide. On election night, Stephen Lewis couldn't hold back the tears; if only he'd known that socialist Valhalla was this close at hand, he wouldn't have told them to take a hike a while back when he could have had the party leadership on a platter, and now he'd be premier of Ontario instead of having to fish for talking-head gigs on Newsworld.

together is the abiding conviction that the rest of us are being bled dry so the Toronto bastards can wallow in the best of everything, though you wouldn't actually want to move there unless it was the sole alternative to imminent starvation. From that point of view, the '90s have been most gratifying for non-residents of Ontario, in that no punishment (with the possible exception of the runaway Alberta favorite that the whole bunch of them should be hogtied and hauled the full length of Yonge St. behind chuckwagons with crack junkies at the reins) could have been more appropriate than what the Ontario electorate visited on itself in this decade by turning its provincial government over to Bob Rae and his Dipper horde of muffinhead socialists.

Peter Kormos demoted for one reason or another

57

But before long he had reason to smile once more and congratulate himself on his good fortune and infallible foresight, and feel grateful it wasn't him being burned in effigy by the brothers and sisters in the public-service unions as they stormed Queen's Park with pitchforks in defence of their inalienable right to lifetime job security on the people's payroll. In a way it was reassuring to know that even socialists have vested interests; when it came to the crunch, it was solidarity forever, or until you mess with big labour's benefit packages. By all accounts, a terrible fate awaits this crowd the next time Ontario goes to the polls, and richly deserved it will be. Any party that can't accommodate a truly fun guy like Peter Kormos, after putting up with the dreary likes of Evelyn Gigantes and "Pink" Floyd Laughren all these years, isn't worthy of the name. This ain't no party, it's a Presbyterian wake.

Cartoonist's note: TorStar editors didn't notice Bourassa's nose in this one

"When one's left wing is not working, one tends to fly around in circles a great deal."

Bob Rae
from the book
POLITICAL
BABBLE

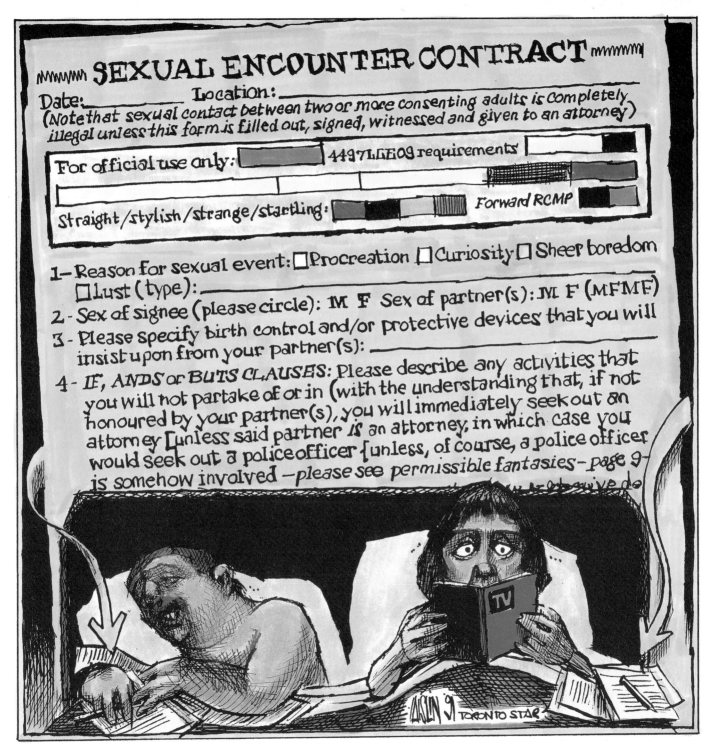

SEXUAL ENCOUNTER CONTRACT

Date:_____ Location:_____

(Note that sexual contact between two or more consenting adults is completely illegal unless this form is filled out, signed, witnessed and given to an attorney)

For official use only: ▨▨▨ 4497LEEOg requirements ▨▨▨

Straight/stylish/strange/startling: ▨▨▨▨ Forward RCMP ▨▨

1 – Reason for sexual event: ☐ Procreation ☐ Curiosity ☐ Sheer boredom
☐ Lust (type):_____

2 – Sex of signee (please circle): M **F** Sex of partner(s): **M** F (MFMF)

3 – Please specify birth control and/or protective devices that you will insist upon from your partner(s):_____

4 – IF, ANDS or BUTS CLAUSES: Please describe any activities that you will not partake of or in (with the understanding that, if not honoured by your partner(s), you will immediately seek out an attorney [unless said partner is an attorney, in which case you would seek out a police officer [unless, of course, a police officer is somehow involved – please see permissible fantasies – page 9 –

AISLIN 91 TORONTO STAR

Chapter 4: The '90s So Far

It's sometimes hard to get a good handle on a decade in its early incarnation. Often a decade's defining characteristics don't really take hold before it's almost half over. What we now remember the '60s for didn't really start happening until after the Beatles appeared on the Ed Sullivan Show and suburban white kids discovered that smoking marijuana made you only a little bit crazy, and, for an added bonus, the very thought of it could drive your parents straight up the curtains. The '70s, which were largely the '60s run to sap, didn't really come into their own until they dragged poor brain-dead Jerry Ford off the golf course and stuck him into the Oval Office, and Western culture was stricken with Saturday Night Fever, which caused its victims to dress like Dade County greaseballs and buy Bee-Gees records by the millions. In Canada it took until Joe Clark wimped into Conservative party leadership and Dan Hill oozed up the pop charts. And while Ronald Reagan was in White House from the very outset of the '80s, the decade began quite out of character with a recession that hardly presaged the lavish corporate feeding frenzy that followed. The '80s acquired their lasting imprimatur of unabashed greed and overpriced vulgarity only after Mike Milken and the Material Girl emerged as defining cultural icons well into the decade.

Looking at it from another perspective, how-ever, it could be said that the '80s weren't ac-tually much more than the '70s with a windfall excess of disposable income to indulge what were essentially the same egregious tastes and bankrupt ethics that gave us Watergate and the doubleknit leisure suit. On the level of mass culture there wasn't much in the way of progression from the Bee-Gees to Phil Collins, for instance, except that the records cost twice as much in the '80s. Trading in Quaaludes for cocaine as the recreational drug of choice wasn't exactly a sign that people were getting any smarter, though it gave a whole new mean-ing, at once literal and figurative, to the concept of blowing one's dough. Looking at it that way, the '90s so far have been pretty much the '80s coming to in a strange hotel room with a crippling hangover and a pocketful of bad poker debts. It's different, but things haven't fundamentally changed all that much. Corporate raiders have been reborn as cor-porate downsizers, but this hardly heralds the dawn of a kinder, gentler age. Instead of stalk-ing each other, they now prey on their own employees; instead of swallowing up each other's companies, they now cannibalize their own. The art of cutting the deal has been over-taken by the art of inflicting the sack. The rich are still getting richer, only more of us seem to be getting poorer, and every year it seems like the month of February somehow lasts a little

But he claims to be participating in the ultimate spiritual Canadian act - collectively, all of us, coping with February, each in our own way...

longer in this country, even though the calendar still claims it has the fewest number of days.

Still, there's been enough accumulation of '90s detritus that sifting through the sand that's run through to the bottom of the glass so far can be a worthwhile exercise, though it's possible, in light of recent precedents, that the next big thing may be just about to come slouching down the pike. (On the other hand, trying to cash in with a book about the decade at this ridiculously early stage could in itself be qualified as a quintessentially '80s scheme. But in the hardscrabble spirit of this decade, we can claim to be motivated more by sincere desperation than shameless avarice. We may have learned our lesson with junk bonds and speculative shares, but we still gotta think RRSP or it'll be catfood and cooking sherry in our rapidly approaching dotage; we've kicked Courvoisier and Peruvian flake, but now the kids have to be put through college or they'll never leave home.)

At this point, the best we can hope for from this decade is that it too will turn out to be a late bloomer, otherwise it's going to be a grim slog to the new millennium. Up to now the decade that the nasty '90s have most often been compared to is the dirty '30s, though mostly by people who didn't actually experience the Great Depression, which was a vastly more unforgiving time, all things considered. The '90s could also do with a bath, but compared to the '30s they're only somewhat smudged. Back then there was no such thing as golden parachutes for corporate failures; it was splat on the pavement for those who took the fall when the market crashed. At the other end of the scale, pogey may be a threadbare substitute for a steady job, but at least this time the armies of the unemployed weren't driven to riding the rails en masse. Not that they could have done so in any case, because there aren't enough trains left running after years of rail service cutbacks to sustain a viable hobo movement.

Indeed, staying home, for better or for worse, has become the thing to do in the '90s. Like most other definitive social trends during the past three decades, it's largely a byproduct of the baby boom generation stumbling on a new phase of life. (Today's young people may have had it up to here with the aging hippies and their overbearing auto-centrism, but tough titty Generation X; at this rate the boomers have the numbers and the clout to impose their self-indulgent generational hegemony for about another quarter century.) The stay-at-home trend took hold near the end of the '80s, when the boomers discovered cocooning, which was really just another pretentious yuppie term for hanging around the house. Never mind that this is what their parents did as a matter of course most evenings at the same stage of their lives. Because the boomers did it with lumpfish caviar, California Chablis and porn videos, they were convinced that they were on to something revolutionary. (This congenital boomer tendency to equate their every new fad or obsession with the invention of the wheel or the discovery that the earth rotates is what really grinds on other generations.)

But during the '90s, the yuppie monicker—derived from young urban professionals—has steadily lost its relevance, because there's nothing really young about these people any more. No amount of tummy tucking, stairmaster workouts and hair replacement can alter the fact that in this decade, middle age is overtaking the youthquake generation with a vengeance. (Warning to Generation Xers: ex-

Saluting: Ordinary Heroes!

MEET MARTY DROOBLES, WHO IS AS ORDINARY AS THEY COME, EXCEPT..!

IN THE PRIVACY OF HIS OWN HOME, WATCHING ENDLESS NUMBERS OF TELEVISION SHOWS — OFTEN ALL AT THE SAME TIME — HE SLOWLY REALIZED THAT GOD GRANTED HIM A SPECIAL GIFT...

MARTY WAS JUST CROWNED 1994 REMOTE CONTROL CHAMP OF THE WORLD!!!

CHAMP

MARTY, RECENTLY DIVORCED (FOR THE THIRD TIME), NOW SHARES A MODEST CO-OP WITH HIS FOUR-TEEN T.V. SETS

AISLIN 94
MONTREAL GAZETTE

pect to hear a lot of agonizing about menopause and colonic disorders for the rest of the decade, and if you find that tiresome and more than slightly nauseating, count your blessings that it'll be a few years yet before they're into incontinence.) Now they're staying home because they're just too whipped by the rat race they once disdained to go out much any more. And if they do, they're liable to run into their kids at the bar with fake ID, which is embarrassing for everyone.

But the new sedentariness is more than just a case of the boomers hitting the geriatric wall. Recent advances in technology are giving all of us fewer reasons to get out of the house, and less occasion to interact directly with fellow human beings. The road that beckons today's adventurous spirit isn't Route 66—which officially disappeared from the maps in this decade—but the information highway. Cyberspace has acquired the lure that uncharted oceans once held for explorers in the days of wooden ships, and a dozen megabytes of RAM in your personal computer can now get you more places than a herd of horses under your hood. Virtual reality devices will soon let us visit exotic locales without leaving our living rooms, or having to drink the local water and be fleeced by marauding airport cab drivers. (Open sewer stench will be optional for those who want to enhance the experience beyond the visual.) People can now talk to each other through their computer screens, or communicate by E mail, voice mail and fax transmissions without having to worry about dressing ap-

propriately or fretting about deodorant failure. They can now have casual sex over the phone, with or without clothes on. Equipped with a Mac, a modem and a phone line, a growing number of people can do their jobs at home, wearing pyjamas and a bathrobe all day long if they want. Thanks to the explosion in telephone technology, half the time we spend on the phone nowadays is with a machine at the other end …

Advances in satellite transmission and reception, combined with the perfection of the remote-control device, is bringing couch-potato culture to its apotheosis. Channel surfing has become the sport of the '90s; the truly adept can circumvent commercials entirely, but this raises the dilemma of when to raid the fridge or go to the bathroom. Though the quality of the content appears to be decreasing in direct proportion to the proliferation of channels, the spectacular range of viewing choices already available, from nonstop fuckflicks to 24-hour-a-day Baptist bible belting, ensures we'll spend more time than ever pinned to the sofa.

The advent of the 500-channel universe in this decade has signalled the demise of the major networks as we knew them. The burgeoning panoply of viewing options has fragmented the TV audience to the point where we're no longer captive to the vapid mainstream pap they've been stuffing down our throats since the invention of the cathode ray tube. Democracy in the electronic global village is bringing junk culture into the age of specialization. Most of it will still be vapid pap—we're talking television here, after all—but there'll be a brand for every fancy. What this implies is that there really isn't a mass audience out there any more in the way there was 30 years ago. Like a giant amoeba, popular culture has sub-divided into so many categories that there may not be another transcendent pop phenomenon like the Beatles in this decade. Much the same audience fragmentation that has eroded the dominance the established TV networks is also evident on the pop charts, where rock and roll is no longer the undisputed king, but merely one of an array of princelings, each with a hardcore constituency. For example, the

- SEVERAL WOMEN WALKED A BREAST
- OTHER WOMEN DEBATED THE ACTION
- STRAIGHT MEN WISELY KEPT THEIR MOUTHS SHUT

Men & women, men & men, women & etc...

"Your honour, my client feels that, by requesting pension benefits for both his legal spouse, Jennifer *and* Mario—their live-in house servant of many years—he will be symbolically establishing legal emancipation, dignity and respect for all practicing bisexuals."

occupants of the Billboard Top 20, as this was being written, ranged from sanforized hillbilly rocker Garth Brooks to nutrasweet pop diva Celine Dion to grunge blasters Soundgarden to bang-'em-out gangsta rappers Snoop Doggy Dog to the Benedictine monks of Santo Domingo de Silos, chanting the greatest hits of the 12th century.

It might just be that the big thing about the '90s is that there won't be any next big thing. Maybe what we're seeing now is what we'll get for the rest of the decade. If so, the '90s promise be a lot like the month of February on a Canadian calendar; they'll last for 10 years like every other decade, but it'll seem like much longer.

A slogan for the latter '90s?

Couple spotted making love in hotel room window overlooking Toronto's Skydome

Pat Burns in...Toronto?

Wayne Gretzky & John Candy buy Argos

CFL expansion planned

GREAT BASEBALL PLAYERS ARE NOT ALWAYS NICE GUYS.

BABE RUTH WAS A NOTORIOUS WOMANIZER...

TY COBB WAS A TERRIBLE RACIST...

HACK WILSON WAS A HOPELESS DRUNKARD...

PETE ROSE BELONGS IN THE HALL of FAME.

COUCH POTATO GOLD...

Chapter 5: As the World Turns

Anti-Americanism is as essential a Canadian staple as maple syrup, durum wheat and frozen tootsies in February. It has been such ever since the Yankees converted Boston Harbor into the world's biggest teapot in a widely misunderstood bid for recognition in the 1773 edition of the Guiness Book of Records that went woefully wrong. Consider what its ongoing repercussions have led to in this decade: Rush Limbaugh; designer grunge; Butthead and Beavis; Branch Davidians and The Nation of Islam; Ross Perot; infomercials; The Bridges of Madison County; Achy-Breaky Heart; wildman weekends; Bubba pride; Camille Paglia; greater Miami; tabloid TV; home video; the Buffalo Bills; Michael Bolton; gangsta rap; political correctness; spray-on hair; stupid pet tricks; the Flintstones movie; Oprah Winfrey's weight chart; and the rehabilitation of Richard Nixon.

Canadians like to pose as the hapless victims of the American junk culture behemoth, as though they make us watch "Murphy Brown" and "Married With Children" at gunpoint when what we really want is more distinctly Canadian stuff that will improve our minds, like "Urban Angel" and "E.N.G." But doth we not protest too much? Haven't we done more than our bit to make American popular culture the vacant shuck it's become in the '90s? Sure we've exported some class acts in our time,

like Oscar Peterson, Leonard Cohen, the Cirque du Soleil, John Kenneth Galbraith and Moosehead lager. But we're far from blameless, as the Can-con propagandists would have us believe. This is, after all, the country that bears responsibility for polluting the continental mainstream with the likes of David Foster, Celine Dion, Graydon Carter III, Michael J. Fox, the Florida Panthers, Shirley, Shannon Tweed, Bryan Adams, CFL expansion teams, the Mackenzie Brothers, Anne Murray, Mort Zuckerman, Robert Goulet, rye and seven, Allan Thicke, Paul Schaefer and Neil Young, the godfather of grunge, whom we can thank for inspiring a whole generation of North American youth to dress like laundromat discard bins.

What really gets the Canadian goat is that we're obsessed with the Americans, while they couldn't care diddly-squat about us, except when some backwoods northwestern state senator goes ballistic over subsidized softwood lumber exports. We've got their number, while they don't even know our area code. Canadians know for fact that Americans are a nation of bourbon-fed rednecks, corporate Visigoths, cultural knuckledraggers, neo-nazi pols and gun-happy sociopaths who'd sooner blow your head off than yield at an intersection. It's upsetting, therefore, that Americans tend to view Canadians in terms of crude

AFTER CAREFUL CONSIDERATION WAS GIVEN TO THE STERN CANADIAN MEMO, ALL THE PRESIDENT'S MEN RETURNED THEIR ATTENTION TO THE N.B.A. FINALS...

CANADA? SURE... BIG!!! FILLED THE WHOLE TOP OF THE MAP...

...CLEAR UP TO THE NORTH POLE.

MOUNTAINS AND LAKES; I'VE GOT POSTCARDS... SOME SAID IT WAS THE MOST BEAUTIFUL COUNTRY IN THE WORLD.

BUT COLD WINTERS, THEY SAY, WHICH MUST HAVE FROZEN THE PEOPLES BRAINS OR SOMETHING.

BECAUSE THEY BROKE THE COUNTRY UP INTO LITTLE BITS & PIECES, ALL OF WHICH...

...THE JAPANESE THEN BOUGHT UP FOR GOLF COURSES AND THINGS.

stereotypes. After all the money we've poured into Canada Council grants in the service of the Canadian identity, the word Canadian, in the average American mind, still evokes little more than images of golden-throated Mounties, vacant space, ale-sucking hosers, cement-headed hockey players, dry ginger ale, rye whisky, and a lifetime supply of ice. Most Canadians can tell you exactly who George Washington was, while most Americans are blissfully ignorant of John A. Macdonald. If pressed, they'll venture that he must be Johnny Walker's Canadian cousin.

The worst is that they don't think we're all that much different from them, except that most of us speak French and live in igloos. For all our paranoid fulminations about the corrupting influence of their rapacious materialism and prodigious bad taste on Canadian society, they persist in thinking that we're the finest neighbours any country could have. Dull as fenceposts maybe, but that's part of our native charm as far as they're concerned; it just makes the pickings easier north of the 49th. As much as we insult them, Americans remain largely convinced that we want most to be more like them, and they're only too eager to help us along. In their benighted arrogance they fail to realize how different we are, and that we like it that way. Who needs Wall St., after all, when we've got Bay St.; or Howard Stern when we've got Don Cherry; or Phil Donahue when we've got Peter Gzowski; or Pat Buchanan when we've got Preston Manning? Still, in our darkest moments of

Hillary and Whitewatergate

introspection we have to admit they may have a certain point. After all, what's "Street Legal" but "L.A. Law" with tackier sets and low-rent talent, and what's the big difference between Peter and Pam and Dan and Connie, apart from a few follicles and a few million bucks (U.S.)?

from the Kuwaiti oilfields recuperation exercise at the beginning of 1991, civil wars have been the order of the decade. The thing to do in the '90s, it seems, is to hate the people who resemble you most closely. In what appears to be a case of Freud's narcissism of minor dif-

And when you get right down to it in your Canadian heart of hearts, isn't Mel Hurtig basically Ross Perot with a maple leaf tattooed on his butt instead of the stars and stripes?

This Canadian hostility against the Americans for heaping us with the detritus of their manifest destiny may go back to the days when Benedict Arnold was a draft dodger. But

Are all those Floridians, recently critical of Quebec tourists, really in a position to lecture les Québécois?

On how to dress?

Wallgreens

On how to speak? On what to eat?

HI Y'ALL! AAM DEBBI, YUR WAYTRISS T'NIGHT, ON A BED UV RICE PILAFF UR A BAKED POTAYTOE

DEEBI

AISLIN '92 TORONTO STAR

On culture?

WE LIVE

I-95 UNDERWATER CONDOS

Uncle Sam's LIKER Store

Surf 'n Turf LITE! DRIVE THRU

DRUGS 'R' US

Federal Jesus Saves Bank

Anita Bryant Muzeum

On dealing with minorities?

GIT BACK T'YR SHACK BOY WHERE THE TOO-RISTS C'AINT SEE YA!

FREE

ference run rampant, we've had Hutus massacring Tutsis in Rawanda, even though they're said to have trouble telling each other apart without birth certificates; warring clans in Somalia; Serbians, Croats and Bosnians slaughtering each other in what they used to share as Yugoslavia; Azerbaidjanis killing Armenians; political factions shelling each

it also puts us right in step with the with the global trend in the '90's. Now that the cold war is over and inter-hemispheric tensions have eased, people throughout the world have increasingly been taking out their aggressive tendencies on their nearest neighbours. Apart

other in Afghanistan and Angola; Crips rumbling Bloods in the streets of L.A.; and Floridians, for God's sake, slagging Quebecers for their garish taste in leisure wear. In the same spirit—though our weaponry is largely restricted to belligerent screeds in *The*

Canadian Forum, earnest *Toronto Star* editorials and zingers from the Royal Canadian Air Farce—the sons of Uncle Sam are the closest thing Canadians have to a serviceable enemy on whom we can vent our national frustrations. Now if they'd only wake up and notice from time to time . . .

Yet the '90s up to now have also been a decade of global reconciliation. Amid the proliferation of fratricidal carnage around the world, there have been historic developments that bode well for mankind. The greater the differences between people, the better the chance that they'd get along in this decade. In the '90s alone, South Africa dismantled the walls of apartheid, and held free elections in which blacks and whites joined to anoint Nelson Mandela as their president; in the Middle East, the Israelis and the Palestinians managed to sign a peace agreement, and Lebanon has disappeared from newscasts; Britain and France put centuries of bitter bygones aside and linked their shores with the "Chunnel," though the Brit navvies couldn't resist sending a frog hopping down the borehole when they broke through to the other side; the Vatican apologized to Galileo, thereby joining the world community in recognizing that the earth is round and revolves around the sun, and can now devote the next four centuries to understanding human sexuality; Russia has resolutely taken the capitalist road under Boris Yeltsin, and is becoming more Americanized every month, though the part of America it most closely resembles at this point is Dodge City, circa 1875.

89

MID-EAST PEACE?...

IT'S A BIRD, IT'S A PLANE!...It's a dove???

OUR FAVORITE NEWS ITEM OF 1992?
The Vatican apologizing to a long-dead Galileo

NEWS ITEM: Pope rejects women ever being ordained as priests

NEWS ITEM: A report in the *National Catholic Reporter* estimates that at least one-third of all Catholic priests are homosexuals...

90

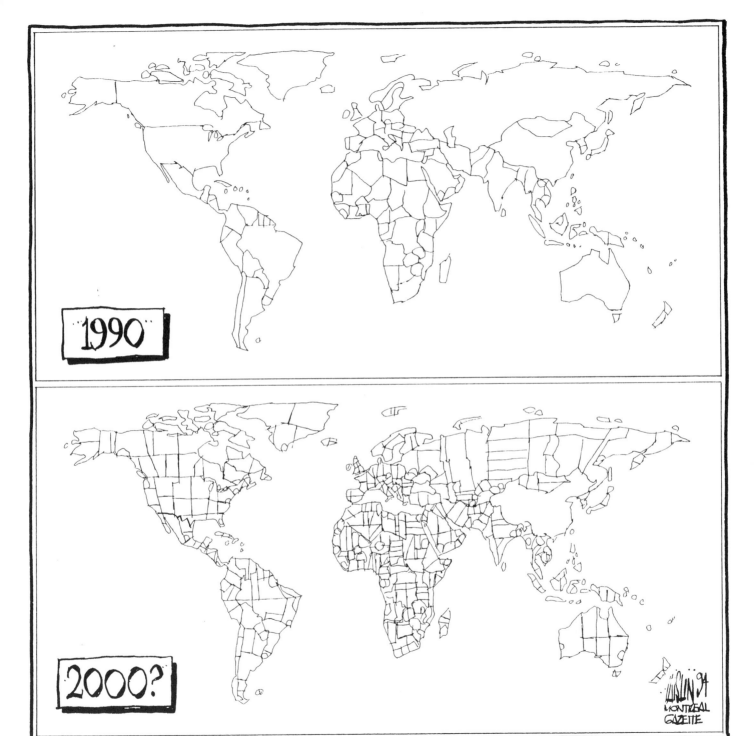

1990

2000?

91

Forgotten Russian cosmonaut spends 10 months in space

Gorbachev invited as observer to G-7 summit

The wars of the '90s have been comparatively restricted atrocities in trivia-question countries that few people care passionately about unless they happen to live there. Except for sending in token relief supplies and hamstrung peacekeeping contingents, the major powers have not let themselves be drawn into these local conflicts, as has happened in the past with monumental global consequences. Eighty years ago it took only one guy getting shot in Sarajevo to touch off a world war; in the '90's, a sizeable portion of the city's population has been annihilated, yet the major powers serenely pressed on with the GATT treaty negotiations. Tensions rose at times, over sticky questions like the floor price of broiler chickens and domestic dairy subsidies, but there was never any serious question of calling up the Marines to make the world a more receptive place for Midwestern grain exports. We appear to have reached the point where the big-hitting countries, whatever racial, linguistic or social differences may divide them, now hold so much of each other's paper that going to war is no longer a practical means of pursuing diplomacy.

There has been a great deal of academic handwringing over the steadfast reluctance on the part of the major powers to do more than dabble halfheartedly in the planet's current hellholes. One bunch of Washington think tank wonks recently blamed it on an attack of "strategic arthritis," which has come to grip the Western powers, notably the U.S., this decade. But it could also be that Western minds have been elsewhere most of the time. Like the bedroom, for instance.

95

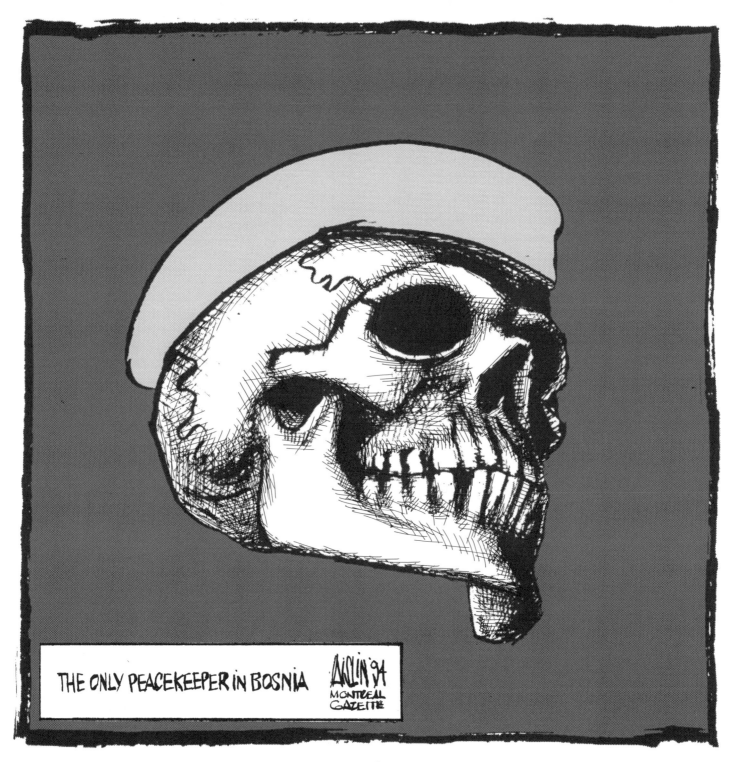

THE ONLY PEACEKEEPER IN BOSNIA — AISLIN '94 MONTREAL GAZETTE

Politics and sex have been inseparable in this decade. On any given day, the political pages of the *New York Times* are liable to concern themselves with the same subject matter as the current *National Enquirer*, though couched in anal-retentive prose. For most Americans, the Clarence Thomas-Anita Hill affair, which apparently didn't get even get as far as hands-on touchy-feelie, was far more riveting than the rape of Vukovar. Bill Clinton's foreign policy was less of a factor for Americans during the '92 presidential election campaign than his alleged weakness for bimbos. There were even suggestions in the serious media that George Bush had a thing with one of his secretaries, though it was hard to convince the general public that anything certifiably bipedal would participate in an unforced sexual relationship with George Bush.

With the floodgates thrown open, we learned that Winston Churchill would fuck women as casually as Harry Truman smoked cigars, and that J. Edgar Hoover, the generalissimo of the G-Men, was actually a closet queen. In Britain, the monarchy was rocked to its foundations by juicy tales of tales of royal bedhopping, complete with published transcripts of the pillow talk, and Prime Minister John Major has lost close to half his cabinet to scandals with a carnal dimension. No wonder the West has been having a hard time getting its act together. It's not easy bringing about a new world order with your mind in the gutter and your pants around your ankles.

The Gulf war was only the exception that proved the general rule. If Kuwait's national

ANOTHER GREAT MOMENT IN HISTORY:
Dressed in traditional garb, the Prime Minister of the newly separated Republic of Northwest Kränko-Azerbastershatsky-dropoffstanslaw greets the recently appointed ambassador from Borisglöblitzûûsrussio-Pyakakorazorñshev...

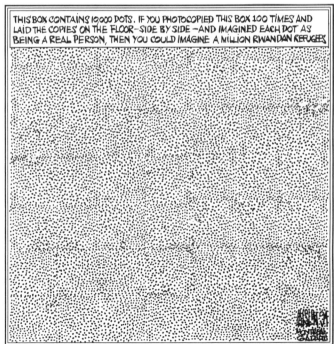

THIS BOX CONTAINS 10,000 DOTS. IF YOU PHOTOCOPIED THIS BOX 100 TIMES AND LAID THE COPIES ON THE FLOOR—SIDE BY SIDE—AND IMAGINED EACH DOT AS BEING A REAL PERSON, THEN YOU COULD IMAGINE A MILLION RWANDAN REFUGEES

product had consisted of cabbages instead of bunker crude, the NATO alliance would have sold the Iraqis harvesting machines and packing crates instead of bombing them back to the stone age. For all the demonization of Saddam Hussein, the Kuwaiti royal family didn't come off as being much more lovable. The major discernable difference between them is that Saddam preferred to sink his petrodollars into tanks and rockets instead of roulette and Rolls Royces. But even so, if the Iraqi invasionhadn't threatened to drive up the pump price for premium unleaded in New Jersey, we would have let Saddam have Kuwait for a firing range and shipped him all the ammunition he needs to get his rocks off. There was a lot of armchair-general hype about Operation Desert Storm being the first high tech-war, as though Saddam and General Schwartzkopf were having it out at Space Invaders in a video arcade. Only later did we learn that most of the microchip guided missiles and so-called smart bombs missed their targets, and that most of the casualties sustained by the Iraqi army were buried alive in their trenches by earth movers.

HOW WARS ARE REMEMBERED...

...HOW WARS ARE.

AISLIN '91
MONTREAL
THE GAZETTE

If Desert Storm proved anything, it was that no matter how much you refine the technology, nothing can take the sheer hell out of war.

LAUGH

AISLIN 91
MONTREAL
THE GAZETTE

99

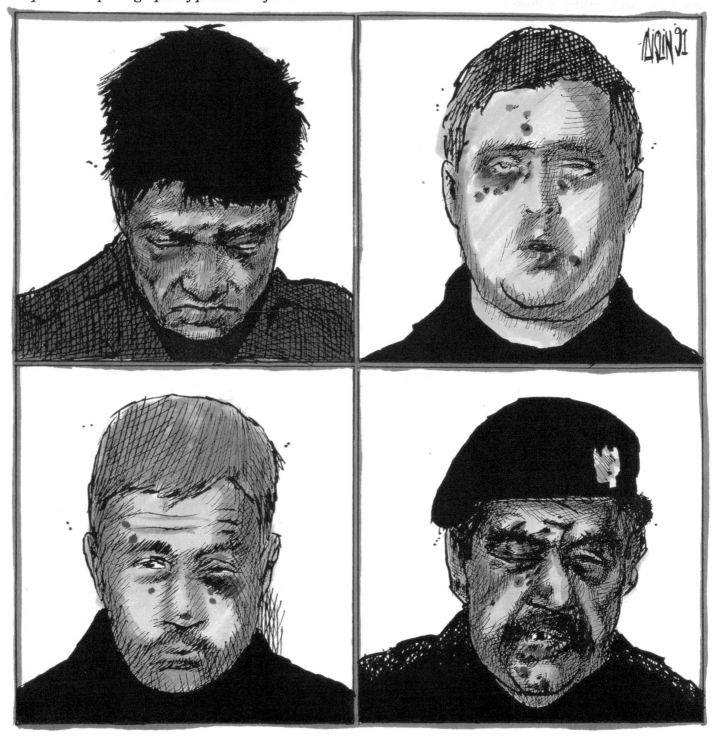

Chapter 6: The End of Brian

"Nice country, nice mess," is how the British high-forehead newsweekly *The Economist* headlined a rare in-depth feature on Canada in the '90s a while ago. The article went on to note that according to prevailing world standards, Canada is singularly rich, peaceful and successful, but somehow feels the need to indulge in petty quarrels that have carried it to the verge of disintegration. It allowed that we're going about this in a typically wholesome Canadian manner, compared to some other fragmenting jurisdictions around the world. Instead of mortars and machine guns, we have at each other with weighty manifestos, bloated rhetoric and bilious rants on open-line shows. The only civilian casualties of our constitutional showdown, which has dominated the country's political agenda in this decade, either perished of ennui or went off their rockers trying to figure out the difference between a normative clause and an interpretive clause, and which of the two is judiciable. But even at that *The Economist* linked us with the late U.S.S.R. and the former Yugoslavia in weighing our prospects for survival as a nation. "What's a nice country like Canada doing in a mess like this?" it wondered.

Maybe it's because we've had it up to here with nice. Maybe we want to develop a global identity with a little more edge than merely nice. Maybe we're jealous of people with a more sharply defined national stereotype, like the snotty English, the tightwad Scots, the libidinous French, the drunken Irish, the ugly Americans, the belligerent Germans, or the inscrutable Japanese. Nice doesn't cut much of a profile in such colourful company.

We always suspect that when foreigners say we're nice, what they really mean is that we're dead boring—a nation that wipes its feet, washes behind its ears, wears sensible shoes, lines up at the bus stop, slows down on the yellow and closes its matchbook cover before striking. Maybe we're tired of being taken for granted as the goody-two-shoes in the dysfunctional family of nations while the delinquent siblings get all the attention. Nice Canadians, eh? Maybe they'll take us more seriously if we flush this nice country right down the toilet!

And whaddya know, it seems to be working. We must be doing something right if

HATING BRIAN?

HEY, MULDOO!

The Economist now has us in the same paragraph as the U.S.S.R and Yugoslavia. And lookee here, don't we have The *Times* of London sitting up and taking notice: "Lucky the land that was once so boring," it pronounced recently, meaning us. "It may have the misfortune to become interesting." Today the *Times* of London, tomorrow *People* magazine; this country's on a roll.

It may not be anything quite so calculated, but there's no denying that the quality of niceness has been sorely strained in Canada during the '90s. Since the beginning of this comedown decade, the national disposition has veered to decidedly un-Canadian extremes of rancor and cynicism. In the fall of 1990, former Ontario premier David Peterson remarked, in what stands up as the understatement of the decade so far: "It seems there's a certain crankiness out there." A year and $26 million later, the Spicer Commission report basically confirmed Peterson's spot diagnosis, though by then we were well past cranky, and bearing down on mad as hell.

Instead of frolicking in the promised fields of free trade clover, we got mugged by a vicious recession that left few Canadian households untouched—the Houses of Parliament being prominent among those spared. In its wake, the concept of rich has been extended to include those with a steady job that doesn't pay too much less than it did a dozen years ago. We've been rudely disabused of the postwar middle-class faith that at the very least the world owes us a bungalow in the burbs with

Anti-Free Trade activist, Maude Barlow (unpublished)

"I forgot — Aren't the last t'leave supposed t'turn out the lights?"

News item: Governments poured more than $100 million into doomed Nova Scotia mine

Life's a... MEECH —then you die.

D'ABORD, M. MULRONEY, CAN THESE ONGOING CANADIAN MOUNTED POLICE INVESTIGATIONS BE POSTPONED UNTIL WE CAN ESTABLISH A SEPARATE QUÉBEC..?

QUÉBECAUCUS

two sets of wheels in the driveway, and we wonder how our kids are going to support us in our old age with the money they make at Macdonald's. The upshot of this decade of diminished expectations is that the future isn't what it used to be.

With the country's economy in a state of incipient collapse, Canada's governing class doggedly applied itself for most of the first two years of the decade to rejigging the constitution, like a crew of addled garage mechanics struggling to rebuild the transmission of a car that was brought in to have its tires rotated. The process culminated in not one, but two overwrought national psychodramas—the Meech Lake ratification fiasco and the Charlottetown referendum blowout—which sapped us of the will to compromise and left the country closer to the breaking point than ever before. Of course, it might have been worse without the constitutional diversion; if our pols had been allowed to spend the whole time cooking the country's books, Canada would likely be washing dishes in the kitchen of the World Bank's executive dining room by now.

Canadians have a reputation abroad for a kind of hangdog deference to authority and the established order that borders on the unhealthy. As a country, we're widely viewed as the good sons of the Western world, who believe our betters know what's good for us, and think the policeman is our friend. From afar we're seen as a nation of trained seals and compulsive teacher's pets. We are not renowned for strong stands or powerful emotions; what makes us nice also renders us wishy-washy in the eyes of the world. Yet in this decade Canadians have turned on their governing class with a scattergun fury that astounded the pollsters and befuddled our complacent power elite. Pollsters reported that never before, or at least not since the discovery of the random sample, have Canadians been as cynical about the system and as contemptuous of mainstream politicians as in the '90s. In a sublime flight of indiscretion, the prime minister's resident polling wizard—R.I.P. Allan (Bomb the Bridges) Gregg—conceded at one point that Canadians no longer trusted their government to run a two-hole outhouse.

To keep things in perspective, this was Brian Mulroney and his Tory administration he was talking about. By this time they'd tested the limits of our vaunted Canadian equanimity by inflicting upon us the likes of Marcel Masse and Sinclair Stevens; Bob Coates and Suzanne Blais-Grenier; Tom Siddon and Roch La Salle; Senator Michel Cogger, Ambassador Lucien Bouchard and Governor-General Ray Hnatyshyn; the tainted tuna scandal and the Oerlikon affair; the GST and the FTA; the Meech Lake boondoggle and the Charlottetown scam; the redecoration tab at 24 Sussex Drive and half a dozen Michael Wilson budgets. By then most Canadians had a ready answer for *The Economist*'s question, and it was two words: Brian Mulroney.

By the '90s, public opinion had soured to the point where everything that went wrong with the country was incarnated in the person of Brian Mulroney. Every dirt farmer's bankruptcy, every

Joe Clark won't run again

111

Eat the POOR! (get a receipt)

widget plant closing, every library funding cut-back and every welfare mother's privation was laid at his doorstep. By the end of his second term, people would curse Brian Mulroney if their cars didn't start on winter mornings, or if their whites didn't come out of the wash whiter than white, or if their chewing gum lost its flavor on the bedpost overnight. A constitutional hotline had to be scrapped when it jammed up with hate calls directed at the prime minister, and Tory pollsters were forced to don protective gear while conducting focus groups with ordinary citizens.

By the time he finally quit, Canadians had worked themselves into such a fervid state of bloody-mindedness over Brian Mulroney and all his works that an Aislin cartoon depicting a bug-eyed Mulroney, sprawled on the pavement in front of his pricey new Westmount retirement digs, tripped up by a whistling Pierre Trudeau strolling in the opposite direction, elicited a wild-ly paranoid response from some of the more rattled Tories, who thought that Mulroney looked decidedly expired in the drawing, and that the walking stick slung over Trudeau's shoulder was actually a rifle. They denounced it

in the House of Commons as an incitement to violence that was liable to give some nut case the idea of going after the prime minister with a shotgun, or at the very least a stick, as though the thought hadn't already occurred to a significant percentage of the country's certifiably sane population.

As it turned out, his prodigious unpopularity was perhaps the most exquisite punishment that could have been inflicted on Brian Mulroney, who suffered the distinction of leaving office as the most intensely despised prime minister in Canadian polling history. Compulsively desperate to be liked and admired, Mulroney was profoundly hurt and thoroughly baffled by the deluge of public hostility that engulfed his administration. In his great generosity of spirit, he had credited Canadians with with a better understanding of how the political process works, and has worked in this country since the days when John A. Macdonald and the railway robber barons laid down the ethical standards of Canada's political culture along with the CPR line.

In light of the enshrined precedents, how could we think for a minute that campaign rhetoric is anything more than hot air, and since when have we started taking politicians' promises seriously? Can there be anyone out there so naive as to expect their leaders to speak the absolute truth at all times? Would anyone ever get elected that way? And wherever did we get this subversive notion that the spoils of power should go to registered charities instead of the prime minister's cronies and the friends of the party? Since when did bagmen and backroom fixers become ineligible for Senate membership? After all, it's how the Liberals operated—o.k., maybe they did it with a little more class and finesse, but that comes with practice—and the Canadian electorate kept them in office for a quarter century straight. What could be more unfair and inconsistent than to deny the Tories an equal chance to fatten themselves on the public feedbag?

Mulroney no doubt wonders to this very day where we suddenly came up with this Sunday school double standard just when it was his turn to cop his rightful due for all the arduous bumlicking, bullshitting and backstabbing it takes to become prime minister. In retirement, he has become a pathetic figure, buttonholing slowfooted rubbies in the streets of downtown Montreal to tell them he could have been more popular than half-priced Molson Ex at happy hour if he'd wanted. "But I made the tough decisions," he mutters over and over as he shuffles along, handing out remaindered copies of his authorized biography to people who drop them into the waste basket at the next intersection.

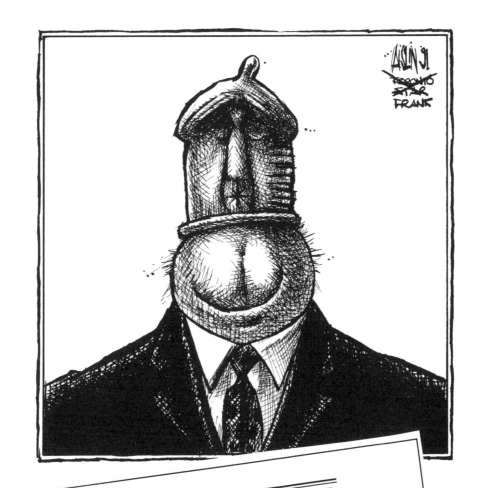

THE TORONTO STAR

From the Editor's desk

Terry:
    Great cartoon!
    But not our cup of tea; try FRANK.

John Honderich

Unpublished

Another Mazankowski budget

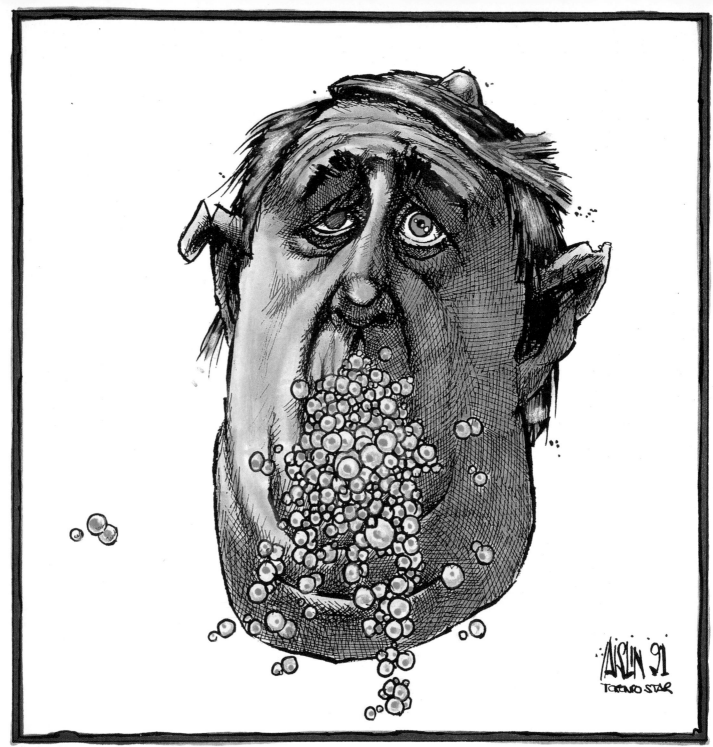

Bubbles 1…

Miss Kimmy

NEWS SHOCKER!... *All Canadians are separated at birth!!!*

Frank McKenna in support of the Yes side

Laurier Lapierre in support of the Yes side

Kim & the Election...

Always the last to catch on to an evolutionary trend, the stonehanded Tories grasped at the notion that our hearts could be sufficiently distracted, and our minds softened enough to forget the preceding nine years, by the novelty of a female prime minister. Either that, or they figured that anything in pants period, down to and including Perrin Beatty, would remind Canadians too much of Mulroney. Never mind that Jean Charest badly outclassed her on the hustings, the Conservatives tossed the party leadership to Kim Campbell, even though her popularity among the general public had been in steady decline since she broke through as a household word in the country by posing for a photographer with her shirt off. It was a cruel joke to play on the women of Canada in particular. As a role model, the country's first female

prime minister ultimately accomplished for Canadian womanhood what Dan Quayle did for North American while males of his generation.

It doesn't seem fair somehow. Israel got Golda Meir, while we got Goldie Hawn with delusions of grandeur; Britain, for better or worse, got Margaret Thatcher, while we got Maggie Muggins with a streak of megalomania.

With the terrible vengeance they wreaked on the Tories in the subsequent federal election, the people of Canada got the last laugh. They may not have trusted them to run one, but they arranged it so the Conservatives could at least hold caucus meetings in a two-holer. In the highest court of natural justice, the verdicts are rendered in pure poetry.

The Media...

Two TorStar NDP columnists

Barbara Frum dies

135

Just too busy to read Quebec's influential newspaper, LE DEVOIR? Here's a handy digest, then, of it's recent diatribes...

> Quack-Quack-Quack-Quack-Quack-Quack-Quack-Quack-Quack-Quack-Quack-Quack-Quack-Quack.
> Quack-Quack-Quack-Quack-Quack-Quack-Quack-Quack-Quack-Quack-Quack-Quack-Quack-Quack-Quack-Rhodesians-Quack-Quack-Quack!
> Quack-Quack-Quack-Quack-Quack-Quack-Quack-Québec-Québec-Québec-Québec-Québec-Québec-Québec-Quack-Quack-Quack-Quack-Quack-Quack.
> Alors, quackons!
> Quack-Québec-Quack-Quack-Quack-Quack-Quack-Quack-Quack-Quack-Quack-Quack-Quack-Québec-Quack-Quack-Quack-Quack.

Lise Bissonnette

AN HONORARY DEGREE IN WHAT?...

Furor over Pierre Peladeau's honorary degree

A suggested tourist attraction: Wherein Montreal's usual commentators would gather at a wall made up of Olympic slabs to wail over the latest slights to the Fatherland...

LINDROS! LINDROCHIEN!

À WOODY'S!

MORDECAI! MORDECAI! MORDECAI!

Slices of life in QuébéCan...
(The first in an occasional series)

"EDITORIALISTS WORKING UP A SWEAT OVER LE DOSSIER LINDROS."

137

A special welcome also, to our distinguished colleagues from the British tabloid Press...

Watney Banger

This legendary Royals correspondent for The Mirror once placed a bugging device in the office of Fergie's gynecologist.

Priscilla Equestrian-Overbite

couldn't write her way out of a paper bag. No matter. She's an expert lip-reader who provides dirty bits on the Royals to a number of London's gossip columns.

Reggie Overhillandale III

Parlayed a drink with Lord Mountbatten during the War into a popular column in The Daily Mail on Nazi war mementoes and accessories.

Mickey Louse - Discovered by

The News of the World shooting porn in Soho, the newspaper then assigned Mickey to photographing Princess Di's wardrobe on windy days.

NEW! WARM BUD

141

Chapter 7: Put Up & Shut Up

Polling has emerged as the most mystical of the political arts in our age. Fundraising, the stuff of so much hoary political legend, is a crude and elementary procedure in comparison: you send some guys out with a bag; they hit on people with fat bank accounts and slip them the suggestion that if they were to fill the bag up with stacks of bills bearing the likeness of Sir Robert Borden, things would go better for everybody. The Gambino family and the Miami syndicate may have patented the technique, but our political parties have refined it to such perfection that hardly anyone complains, and those who do are easily brushed off as obstreperous cranks. (The bag routine is supplemented by the direct mail method, whereby you send studiously crafted begging letters with self-addressed return envelopes enclosed to a selectively targeted index of party members, PTL Club adherents and psychiatric wing outpatients, on the assumption that a fair percentage of each group will send you money thinking that they're paying their cable bills.) A good portion of the cash that political parties amass in this fashion goes to hiring pollsters, whose major function is to tell them how to spend the rest of the loot in a manner that will put their most cynical pitch across as unblushing sincerity.

Pollsters are the latter-day shamans of medi-a age politics, who jolly the cryptic oracle of public opinion for hints of how we can best be manipulated. Nobody likes them very much—not even the people who rent them by the hour—but everyone planning to sell something to the amorphous mass of the great unwashed, from a sanitary product to a political commodity, now feels an absolute need to have one on standby. They are regarded with a mixture of resentment and suspicion by the more linear backroom mechanics, who still believe that if it's results you want, you can do better than a four per cent margin of error 19 times out of 20 with the more tried and manly skills of political enterprise, like packing halls, twisting arms, padding membership lists, dispensing payola and calling the fire department when all else fails.

But even though they come up with the occasional howling clunker that shows the Natural Law Party poised to sweep Alberta, or Lucien Bouchard leading in P.E.I., or the consuming public eager for a brand of PCB-flavoured breath mints, the pollsters, like imperial wizards in a medieval court, have today's pols under their spell. In his scathing book on pollsters, Canadian journalism's last angry man, Claire Hoy, lamented that polls have become the new gods of politics. If so, these gods must be stone crazy, or, at best, beset by a worrisome touch of schizophrenia.

~ WHAT'S THIS BOX STUCK UP IN THE CORNER USED FOR?

I❋I Revenue Canada
Customs, Excise and Taxation

Revenu Canada
Accise, Douanes et Impôt

ANARCHISTS!!!

Federal Individual Income Tax Return for ~~Residents of Quebec~~ ➛

Step 1 – Identification

Attach your identification label here. If you did not receive one or if the information shown is incorrect, print your name and address below.

First name and initial
OTHERWISE

Last name
ENGAGED

Address
GENERAL DELIVERY

City
DYSFUNCTIONAL HOME

Province or territory
NEBULOUSNESS

Postal code
KISOFF

Enter the social insurance number only if the number shown on the label is not correct, or if you are not attaching a label:

Yours: [tic-tac-toe grids]

Your spouse's: [tic-tac-toe grids]

A spouse may include a common-law spouse; see the guide.

Your date of birth: Day Month Year **SCORPIO-LEO**

On December 31, 1993, you were:
1 **YES** Married   2 **YES** Living common-law   3 **NOT YET SOON** Widowed
4 **YES** Divorced   5 **YES** Separated   6 Single

Name of your spouse(s):
BERNICE/SYLVIE/ANDREA/SUE/SAM

Your province or territory of residence on December 31, 1993:
I THINK I WAS STUCK IN O'HARE AIRPORT ALL THAT DAY

If you were self-employed in 1993, state the province or territory of self-employment:
KEY WEST

If you became or ceased to be a resident of Canada in 1993, give the date of:

Entry: Day **SE** Month **PA**   or departure: Day **RA** Month **TIST**

If the individual is deceased, give the date of death: Day Month Year **DEAD ATHEISTS DON'T DO TAXES**

Do not use this area [footprints]

Step 2 – Goods and services tax credit application (See Step 2 in the guide to find out if you should apply.)

Are you applying for the goods and services tax credit?   (Limit one claim per family)   Yes ☐   No ☐

OH, I DUNNO... WHAT'S IN IT FOR ME? GET BACK TO ME ON THIS NEXT FALL, OKAY?

Number of children under age 19 on December 31, 1993 (if applicable)

Enter your spouse's net income from line 236 of your spouse's return (if applicable)   **SEE LINE 236!**

Step 3 – Calculation of total income

Employment income (box 14 on all T4 slips)		101	**I'M**
Commissions (box 42 on all T4 slips)	102		
Other employment income (see line 104 in the guide)		104	**MAD**
Old Age Security pension (box 18 on the T4A(OAS) slip)		113	**AS**
Canada or Quebec Pension Plan benefits (box 20 on the T4A(P) slip)		114	**HELL**
Disability benefits included on line 114 (box 16 on the T4A(P) slip)	152		
Other pensions or superannuation (see line 115 in the guide)		115	**AND**
Unemployment Insurance benefits (box 14 on the T4U slip)		119	**NOT**
Taxable amount of dividends from taxable Canadian corporations (attach a completed Schedule 5)		120	**GOING**
Interest and other investment income (attach a completed Schedule 5)		121	**TO**
Net partnership income: limited or non-active partners only (attach a completed Schedule 5)		122	**TAKE**
Rental income Gross 160 Net		126	**THIS**
Taxable capital gains (attach a completed Schedule 3)		127	**ANY**
Alimony or maintenance income		128	**MORE**

AISLIN '94
MONTREAL GAZETTE

145

Perhaps the definitive poll of Canadian attitudes in the '90's was an Angus Reid survey conducted on the occasion of Canada's 125th birthday in 1992: "Happy Canadians hate everything," said the headline over the report on the poll, in which more than 85 per cent of the respondents expressed general contentment with their lives. At the same time, they indicated that they loathed their entrenched political class, held out little hope for a better future, felt helpless about the desecration of the country's environment, and despair for the nation's young people, whose devalued prospects make it unlikely they'll ever be able to afford the bountiful lifestyle most of us once took for granted, or to have those hideous tattoos removed when they go out of fashion—at about the time their own kids start making fun of them.

A majority of Canadians would probably strongly agree, agree, or somewhat agree that the trials of Job were about as strenuous as Paddington Bear's picnic compared to the staggering run of hardship and misfortune this country has endured in the '90s. Yet, at the same time as bemoaning our unjustly diminished lot became the national pastime, most Canadians, in any given poll, would have emphatically endorsed the proposition that they live in the best country on the planet, which says a lot about our world view, as well as our ambivalent state of mind. (In another Angus Reid probe this decade, 84 per cent of a scientific sample of average Canadians said they'd turn down an offer to move somewhere else; in a similar survey conducted in Britain, close to half the respondents indicated they'd kiss the Sceptred Isle goodbye in a wink if given a chance.)

Less than three months before the Canadian

electorate butchered the Tories in the '93 federal election—the only kind of poll that's always on the money—a representative sample of that same voting public indicated to the Gallup crunchers that Kim Campbell was the country's most popular prime minister since Lester Pearson, back when he was still coasting on his Nobel Prize for fixing the Suez Crisis. Going into that election, barely a quarter of us thought Jean Chrétien had the right stuff to be prime minister, but we still handed the Liberals a strapping majority government.

Six months later, more than 60 per cent of us expressed satisfaction with his performance in office, even though by this time he'd let the black market set the price of cigarettes, given us a cabinet clapped together with midway geek show material like Ron Irwin, Dave Dingwall, André Ouellet, Sheila Copps and Sergio Marchi; suffered the embarrassment of Jag Baduria, caved in to the Yanks on NAFTA, caricatured welfare recipients as beersoaked layabouts, appointed his nephew as ambassador to Washington, and still hasn't become fluent in any known official language. If pollsters were weathermen—*pace* Bob Dylan, in this era of the fragmenting mass audience you do need one to know which way the wind blows—the synopsis for Canada in the '90s would be overcast and variable.

If inconsistency and inherent contradiction are the hallmarks of the Canadian mindset, Quebecers are the most exemplary of all Canadians. No serious public-opinion survey in the province has ever come up with a majority

Lucien Bouchard in Paris promoting Quebec sovereignty

MYSTERIOUS OBJECT CRASHES TO EARTH IN QUEBEC...

Unpublished

in favour of actually separating from Canada. Yet the polling trend for most of the decade has indicated that Quebecers were gearing up to elect the Parti Québécois as their provincial government, though its very *raison d'être* is to hustle the province out of Confederation within the shortest time possible. Quebecers gave Lucien Bouchard and the Bloc Québécois enough of their votes in '93 to install them as Her Majesty's Loyal Opposition in the federal Parliament, though their mission also is to break up the country, the sooner the better.

On the eve of this fateful Quebec election, the conventional wisdom imparted by the almighty polls was that even if Quebecers take a flyer on the separatists in the election, they'll play their hole card by voting against independence in the referendum the PQ has promised to hold within a year. Not surprisingly, there are conflicting interpretations of this highwire instinct on the part of the Québécois to hedge their political bets and play one level of government off against the other—Pierre Trudeau, for instance, never won more seats in Quebec than when Réné Lévesque was premier.

There are some who maintain that this makes Quebecers the canniest and most sophisticated voters in the country, playing the political percentages with the acumen of Jimmy the Greek working the big board in Vegas; in the high-stakes game of federal-provincial poker, they are the Cincinnati Kid. Others regard it as the curse of a people with a profoundly split personality, whose insecurity is such that they can't make up their minds whether to go with the belt or the

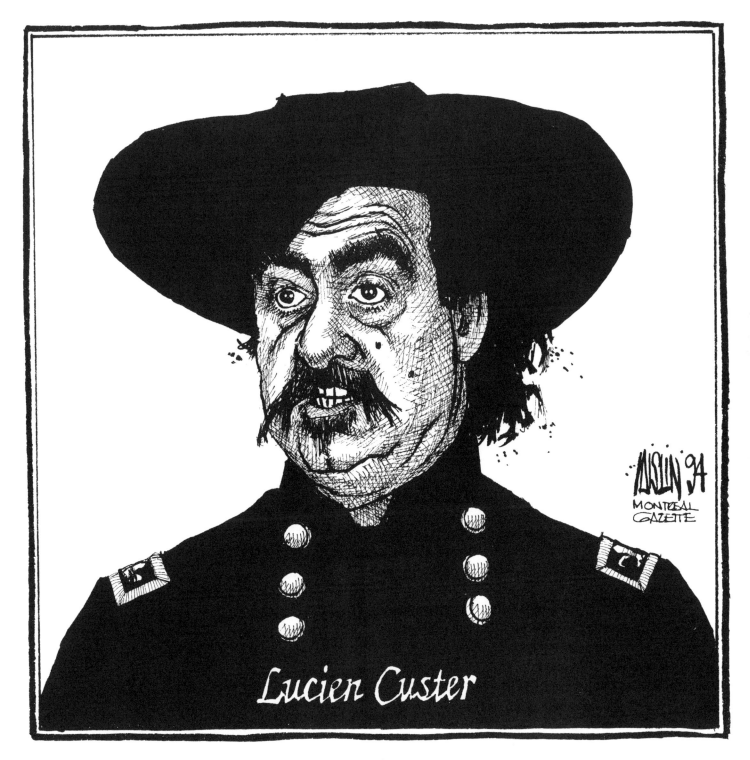

Lucien Custer

suspenders while getting dressed in the morning. "How can you be for the PQ, but against independence?" wondered Richard Martineau, editor of *Voir*, Montreal's French-language alternative weekly paper. "Can you be in favour of Marxism, but oppose the class struggle? For the Catholic church and against the resurrection of Christ?"

Maybe not when you think about it, but in the distinct society, that's nothing to get hung about. Run a poll that asks the right questions, and you'll find that a lot of Quebecers would also agree that you can hate the English, but still love Elvis; be a patriot and pay the plumber under the table; like music and listen to Pink Floyd; mix orange plaid with lime-green polyester; take Jacques Parizeau seriously, and feel *bien chez nous* in Hollywood Beach, Fla. The most

cherished Québécois constitutional preference is special status with the same rights as all Canadians; their idea of a balanced ticket is Dr. Jekyll for prime minister and Mr. Hyde for premier. Their favourite song may indeed be Gilles Vigneault's *Gens du pays*, but running a close second is Joni Mitchell's *Both Sides Now*.

Like deities since time immemorial, the poll gods are untroubled by the constraints of terrestrial logic and the banalities of temporal fact. Polls in this decade have identified law enforcement as a bugbear worthy of mounting hysteria, though crime statistics are in general decline; they would have had us rip up the free trade agreement just when Canadian exports to the U.S. were hitting record highs; they keep francophone Quebecers at a paranoid simmer about losing their language, though more people than ever speak French in the province, and they fooled the

SO, WHAT *IS* ACCEPTABLE DOWN AT THE LEGION AS HEAD-WEAR?

BLIND-AS-A-WALLEYE BALL CAPS...

...DUNCE TOUQUES

OLD, DEAD SKUNKS...

...AND, IF WE HAD OUR WAY

AISLIN '94 MONTREAL GAZETTE

Taxes slashed on cigarettes

Le dollar à 69 cents?

Les économistes de la CIBC prévoient une baisse marquée de la monnaie canadienne

SERGE TRUFFAUT
LE DEVOIR

Le dollar canadien va plonger sous la barre des 70 cents américains au cours des prochains mois, soutiennent les économistes de la CIBC, deuxième institution financière au pays, dans leur dernière analyse.

Après évaluation des tendances qui ont cours actuellement aux États-Unis et au Canada, M. Joshua sohn, économiste en chef de la CIBC, en conclusion que le torique de

CANADA IS A NATION OF 26,000,000 VILLAGE IDIOTS, ALL OF WHOM SWORE THEY'D NEVER BE SUCKERED BY POLITICIANS AND JOURNALISTS INTO ANOTHER NATIONAL UNITY DEBATE EVER AGAIN...

Tories into holding a referendum on the Charlottetown scheme by leading them to believe that Canadians were ready to endorse anything that would put a wrap on the constitutional farce.

The fallacy of relying on polls, no matter how scrupulous their methodology, as a guide for enlightened governance, is that most people pay such scant attention to public affairs that their political opinions are largely an inchoate mash of blinkered self-interest, half-baked prejudices, simplistic dogma and superficial fixations. To keep polls in perspective, it should be kept in mind, given the country's alarming adult illiteracy rate, that roughly a quarter of any truly representative national sample of Canadians can't read a complete sentence. Though the federal deficit was touted as the pivotal issue in the last election, surveys found that barely one Canadian in four had a clear idea of what a budgetary deficit entails, never mind a considered opinion as to whether it should best be eliminated in three years or five years, or simply reduced to a sustainable percentage of GNP. Expecting the Canadian electorate to render a fully informed and closely reasoned judgment on something as complex and convoluted as the Charlottetown contraption was like asking the average citizen to perform emergency neurosurgery upon graduation from a St. John's Ambulance first aid course. For enough people to make the difference in the final count—and the course of Canadian history—it came down to a godsent opportunity to stick it to Brian Mulroney. *Vox populi, vox dei.*

It's understandable, therefore, that the '90s have given rise to the defective twins of contemporary Canadian politics, Lucien Bouchard and Preston Manning, as people cast about for an al-

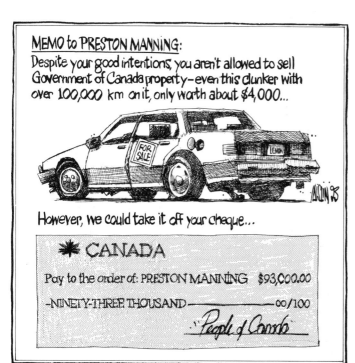

ternative to the established parties. Both, in their own way, embody the decade's disjointed *Zeitgeist*. What could be more in synch with the spirit of this time than a band of Quebec separatists in federal seats, who demand independence, but can't bring themselves to forsake the Canadian dollar? And take Preacher Preston—oh please, sweet Jesus, if you're really out there somewhere—a quintessential '90s guy if there's been one so far: a cowtown nerd proposing to transform this fallen country into a (celestial horns and showers of cherubim) NEW CANADA, by squeezing it into a second-hand Social Credit Sunday-best suit with a few Jiffy-Sew alterations; a populist with a disciplinarian bent, and a ram-rod ideologue who insists the people must decide.

AND SUPPOSE YOU HAD TO CHOOSE BETWEEN LIVING IN A SEPARATE QUEBEC UNDER JACQUES PARIZEAU—OR IN CANADA UNDER PRESTON MANNING?...

EASY CHOICE... BOSTON

To their credit, serious pollsters don't claim to be able to predict the future, and neither should scribes and cartoonists, though none of us mind terribly that there are impressionable souls out there labouring under that delusion. At best they'll hand you fat consulting contracts, at worst they'll buy you rounds in bars and pop the eternal political question that everyone wants answered: "So what's gonna happen?"

Well, to be perfectly honest, we don't know. Not me, and not even the guy who draws the pictures, though we suspect—based on what the '90s have put up so far—that it's going to involve a lot of weirdness and confusion. Stripped of all chrome and bullshit, that's about as good as you'll get from anyone, be it a pollster or a palmreader—Angus Reid or Madame Ru—a tote-board punter or an Ottawa pundit. It's about as far out as we'll venture on what the rest of the decade holds. We don't take ourselves for gods, after all, if only because we like to think we're not that crazy.

So we'll shut up, and let it happen, and get back to you later. . .

...and starts stopping where?